ChatGPT: The Definitive Guide

Master Every Feature — From Your First Conversation to Agent Mode, Deep Research, and Beyond

Ken Tannenbaum

2026

Finnoybu Press

ChatGPT: The Definitive Guide

2026 Edition

Master Every Feature — From Your First Conversation to Agent Mode, Deep Research, and Beyond

---

Published by Finnoybu Press

For permissions and inquiries: press@finnoybu.org

First Edition: 2026

About the Author

Ken Tannenbaum is a technologist, entrepreneur, and AI governance researcher. He is the founder of Finnoybu Press and the founder/steward of the AEGIS Initiative, an open framework for AI safety and accountability. Learn more at aegis-initiative.com.

When he's not building governance standards for artificial intelligence, he's helping everyday people understand and use it.

Dedication

For my family — my purpose in life. I, B & D, R, W, A — I love you all. I could've done it without you, but I honestly wouldn't have wanted to.

And for everyone who typed their first message into ChatGPT and thought, *"What else can this thing do?"* This book is the answer.

The AI for Everyone Series

This book is part of the **AI for Everyone** series by Finnoybu Press, designed to help real people use AI tools effectively. Visit **press.finnoybu.org** for the latest titles and updates.

Collection One: Product Deep Dives

- *ChatGPT: The Definitive Guide (2026 Edition)*
- *ChatGPT: The Power User Guide (2026 Edition)*
- *Claude: The Definitive Guide (2026 Edition)*
- *Claude Code: The Power User Guide (2026 Edition)*
- *Gemini: The Complete Guide (2026 Edition)*
- *Gemini: The Advanced Guide (2026 Edition)*
- *Copilot: The Workplace AI Guide (2026 Edition)*
- *Copilot: The Advanced Workplace Guide (2026 Edition)*
- *Perplexity: The Research Playbook (2026 Edition)*
- *Perplexity: The Advanced Research Playbook (2026 Edition)*

Collection Two: Product Guides

- *NotebookLM: From Sources to Audio Overviews (2026 Edition)*
- *DeepSeek: Code, Math, and Reasoning (2026 Edition)*
- *Cursor: The AI Code Editor (2026 Edition)*
- *OpenClaw: Agentic AI for Everyday Work (2026 Edition)*

Collection Three: Cross-Platform Skills

- *AI Systems Playbook (2026 Edition)*
- *AI Prompt Engineering (2026 Edition)*
- *AI for Developers (2026 Edition)*
- *AI for Business (2026 Edition)*
- *AI for Students (2026 Edition)*
- *AI Governance for Practitioners (2026 Edition)*
- *Securing Agentic AI (2026 Edition)*

Table of Contents

Introduction

I wrote this book because most ChatGPT guides fall into one of two categories: too shallow (a listicle of "top 10 prompts" that barely scratches the surface) or too technical (written for developers and AI researchers, not the rest of us).

Neither serves the person who just wants to understand what this tool can do and how to use it well.

ChatGPT is, by some measures, the most rapidly adopted technology in human history. Within two years of launch, it became a daily tool for hundreds of millions of people. Yet most of those users — even daily ones — use only a fraction of what it offers. They type a question, get an answer, and move on. They don't know about Agent Mode, Deep Research, Projects, Canvas, Study Mode, or the dozens of other features that transform ChatGPT from a clever chatbot into a productivity platform.

This book changes that.

Who This Book Is For

This book is for anyone who uses — or wants to use — ChatGPT. That includes:

- **Complete beginners** who haven't created an account yet
- **Casual users** who use it occasionally but feel like they're missing something
- **Daily users** who want to understand the full feature set
- **Professionals** who want to integrate ChatGPT into their work
- **Students** looking for an effective study tool
- **Business leaders** evaluating ChatGPT for their organization
- **Anyone curious** about what AI assistants can actually do in 2026

You don't need any technical background. If you can type and have a conversation, you already have the skills you need.

How to Read This Book

The book is organized in eight parts that progress from fundamentals to advanced use:

Part I: Getting Started (Chapters 1–5) takes you from zero to your first productive conversations. Even experienced users will likely find features they've overlooked.

Part II: Core Skills (Chapters 6–9) covers the four areas where most people use ChatGPT: writing, research, everyday tasks, and professional work.

Part III: Creative Tools (Chapters 10–12) explores image generation, video creation, and collaborative editing.

Part IV: Productivity Tools (Chapters 13–23) is the largest section, covering every major feature: vision, voice, data analysis, web search, Agent Mode, automation, Projects, custom GPTs, integrations, memory, and the Atlas browser.

Part V: Getting Better Results (Chapters 24–26) teaches prompting techniques, strategies for complex tasks, and output formatting.

Part VI: ChatGPT for Your World (Chapters 27–29) provides targeted guidance for students, businesses, and creators.

Part VII: Safety, Ethics, and Limitations (Chapters 30–32) covers what ChatGPT gets wrong, how to protect your privacy, and the ethical questions worth thinking about.

Part VIII: Reference (Appendices A–F) gives you shortcuts, 75+ prompt templates, troubleshooting, a glossary, a 2026 changelog, and further resources.

You can read straight through or jump to the chapters that interest you most. Each chapter stands on its own, but they build on each other when read in order.

A Note About Accuracy

ChatGPT changes constantly. OpenAI ships updates weekly, sometimes daily. Features get added, interfaces get redesigned, models get upgraded. This book is accurate as of May 2026, but specific details — menu locations, exact pricing, feature availability — may have shifted by the time you read this.

The principles, techniques, and strategies in this book have a much longer shelf life than the specific interface details. How to write an effective prompt, how to verify AI output, how to structure complex tasks — those skills transfer across versions and even across different AI tools.

When something seems different from what's described here, check OpenAI's help center at help.openai.com for the latest information.

Let's Get Started

ChatGPT is the most versatile tool most people have ever had access to. It can help you write, research, learn, create, analyze, plan, and automate — all through nothing more than a conversation.

The only limit is knowing what to ask for.

Turn the page. Let's fix that.

Part I: Getting Started

"The best way to predict the future is to invent it."

— Alan Kay

Chapter 1: What Is ChatGPT?

On November 30, 2022, a San Francisco-based AI research company called OpenAI quietly released a free tool called ChatGPT. Within five days, a million people had tried it. Within two months, it had a hundred million users — by some measures, the fastest-growing consumer application in history.

If you're reading this book, you've probably heard of ChatGPT. You may have tried it once or twice and been impressed, confused, or both. You may use it every day and still feel like you're only scratching the surface. Or you may be picking it up for the first time.

Whatever brought you here, this chapter will give you a clear understanding of what ChatGPT is, how it works, and what it can — and can't — do for you.

What ChatGPT Is

ChatGPT is a conversational AI assistant made by OpenAI. You type a question or request in plain English (or dozens of other languages), and it responds with text that reads like it was written by a knowledgeable human.

That's the simple version. Here's a slightly more complete one:

ChatGPT is powered by a *large language model* — a type of artificial intelligence trained on an enormous amount of text from books, websites, articles, and other sources. Through that training, it learned patterns in how humans use language: how sentences are structured, how ideas connect, how questions typically get answered, and how different tones and styles work.

When you send ChatGPT a message, it doesn't search a database for the answer. It generates a response word by word, predicting the most likely and most helpful next word based on what it learned during training and everything you've said so far in the conversation.

This is why ChatGPT can do things traditional software can't. It doesn't follow a fixed script. It can write a poem, explain quantum physics to a ten-year-old, draft a legal contract, help you debug code, plan your vacation, or brainstorm names for your new business — all in the same conversation.

What ChatGPT Is Not

Understanding what ChatGPT *isn't* matters as much as understanding what it is. Clearing up these misconceptions early will save you frustration later.

ChatGPT is not a search engine. When you ask it a question, it doesn't go look up the answer on the internet (unless you specifically ask it to search). Its responses come from patterns learned during training. That means it can sometimes give you confident-sounding answers that are completely wrong — a phenomenon called *hallucination* we'll cover in detail in Chapter 30.

ChatGPT is not a person. It doesn't have feelings, opinions, or consciousness. When it says "I think" or "I believe," it's using language patterns, not expressing thought. It's a tool — an extraordinarily capable one, but a tool.

ChatGPT is not always right. This bears repeating because it's the single most important thing to understand. ChatGPT presents incorrect information with the same confidence as correct information. It can make up facts, invent citations, and produce plausible-sounding nonsense. Always verify anything important.

ChatGPT is not a replacement for expertise. It's an assistant, not a substitute for a doctor, lawyer, financial advisor, or any other professional. It can help you prepare for a conversation with an expert, but it shouldn't be the final word on decisions that affect your health, finances, or legal standing.

A Brief History

ChatGPT didn't appear out of thin air. It's the result of years of research into language models, and a brief history helps you see both its capabilities and its limitations.

The GPT Series

OpenAI's journey began with a series of models called GPT — short for *Generative Pre-trained Transformer*. Don't worry about what that means technically. What matters is the trajectory:

- **GPT-1 (2018):** A proof of concept. It could generate text, but not usefully or coherently.

- **GPT-2 (2019):** A major step forward. It could write paragraphs that sounded remarkably human. OpenAI initially withheld a public release, fearing misuse for misinformation.
- **GPT-3 (2020):** A leap in capability. With 175 billion parameters (the internal settings the model uses to process language), it could write essays, answer questions, translate languages, and even generate basic code.
- **GPT-3.5 (November 2022):** The model behind the original ChatGPT. It paired GPT-3's language abilities with a conversational interface and fine-tuning that made it helpful and safe. This is what launched the AI revolution.
- **GPT-4 (March 2023):** A significant upgrade in reasoning, accuracy, and the ability to follow complex instructions. It could also process images — a capability called *multimodal* input.
- **GPT-4o (May 2024):** The "o" stands for "omni." It brought voice, vision, and text into a single, faster model that could see, hear, and speak.
- **o1 and o3 (late 2024–early 2025):** A parallel line of reasoning-focused models that took extra "thinking" time before responding. Their approach was later absorbed into GPT-5.4 Thinking.
- **GPT-5 (August 2025):** OpenAI's strongest model to date, with major improvements in writing quality, coding ability, and reduced hallucinations. It introduced better instruction following and far less sycophancy (the tendency to agree with the user even when the user is wrong).
- **GPT-5.3 and GPT-5.4 (2025–2026):** The current generation. GPT-5.3 Instant is the default model for all ChatGPT users, with a single auto-switching system that combines the best capabilities. GPT-5.4 Thinking is the frontier reasoning model, excelling at complex math, coding, document analysis, and agentic workflows.

From Chatbot to Platform

The most important thing to understand about ChatGPT's evolution isn't just that the models got smarter. It's that ChatGPT has transformed from a simple chatbot into a full platform.

The original ChatGPT could only do one thing: have text conversations. Today's ChatGPT can:

- **See** — analyze photos, screenshots, documents, and handwritten notes
- **Hear and speak** — have real-time voice conversations with natural-sounding speech
- **Create images** — generate illustrations, logos, and visual content with DALL-E
- **Create videos** — produce short video clips with Sora
- **Browse the web** — search the internet and provide cited, up-to-date answers
- **Run code** — execute Python, analyze data, create charts, and process files
- **Take action** — use Agent Mode to complete tasks on your behalf using a virtual computer
- **Browse with you** — the Atlas browser puts ChatGPT alongside you as you browse the web
- **Remember you** — retain information across conversations to personalize its responses
- **Work on your files** — connect to Google Drive, OneDrive, and other cloud services

This is no longer just a chatbot. It's a general-purpose AI assistant that handles a remarkable range of tasks. Understanding the full scope of what it can do is what the rest of this book is about.

How It Works (In Plain English)

You don't need to understand the technical details to use ChatGPT effectively, any more than you need to understand internal combustion to drive a car. But a basic mental model helps you get better results and explains why it behaves the way it does.

Training

Before ChatGPT can talk to you, it goes through an extensive training process:

1. **Pre-training:** The model reads an enormous amount of text — books, websites, articles, code repositories, and more. It doesn't memorize this text. It learns patterns: how words relate to each other, how arguments

are structured, how different topics connect. Think of it like a student who has read thousands of textbooks. They don't remember every sentence, but they've absorbed a deep understanding of many subjects.

2. **Fine-tuning:** After pre-training, the model is further trained on examples of helpful, harmless conversations. Human trainers demonstrate what good responses look like, and the model learns to be helpful, honest, and safe.

3. **Reinforcement Learning from Human Feedback (RLHF):** Human evaluators rank different responses to the same question, and the model learns to prefer the kinds of answers humans rate highly. This is what makes ChatGPT helpful and conversational rather than just technically capable.

The Conversation

When you chat with ChatGPT, here's what happens behind the scenes:

1. You type a message.
2. Your message, along with the entire conversation history, is sent to OpenAI's servers.
3. The model processes everything and generates a response one word (actually one *token*, which is roughly three-quarters of a word) at a time.
4. Each new word is chosen based on the model's training and the context of the current conversation.
5. The response streams back to you in real time — that's why you see the text appear gradually.

The Context Window

One of the most important concepts to understand is the *context window* — the amount of text the model can "see" at once, including both your messages and its responses in the current conversation.

Think of it as working memory. Everything within the context window is available for the model to reference. Once a conversation exceeds the window, earlier messages start to fade from the model's attention. This is why long conversations can feel like ChatGPT has "forgotten" what you said earlier.

It's a fundamental architectural limitation, not a bug. We'll cover strategies for managing long conversations in Chapter 25.

What ChatGPT Is Good At

ChatGPT excels in a wide range of tasks. Here are the areas where it consistently delivers strong results:

Writing and editing. ChatGPT is an exceptional writing assistant. It can draft emails, articles, reports, social media posts, cover letters, and creative work. It's particularly good at adapting tone — give it the same content and ask for a formal version, a casual version, and a humorous version, and you'll get three distinctly different pieces of writing.

Explaining complex topics. Ask ChatGPT to explain something and specify your level of understanding. "Explain blockchain like I'm five" produces a very different response from "Explain blockchain to a software engineer." That makes it an excellent learning tool.

Brainstorming and ideation. ChatGPT is tireless. Need fifty names for a bakery? Twenty angles for a marketing campaign? Ten ways to restructure your team? It won't run out of ideas, and it won't judge the ones you suggest.

Coding and technical work. ChatGPT can write, explain, debug, and refactor code in dozens of programming languages. Even if you're not a programmer, it can help you automate tasks, create spreadsheet formulas, or build simple tools.

Analysis and summarization. Give it a long document and ask for a summary. Upload a spreadsheet and ask for insights. Paste in a contract and ask it to highlight the key terms. ChatGPT distills large amounts of information into clear, concise takeaways.

Translation and language. It translates between dozens of languages with impressive accuracy, and it understands idioms, formal vs. informal registers, and cultural context.

Planning and organization. Trip itineraries, project plans, meeting agendas, study schedules — ChatGPT can structure your thinking and turn vague goals into concrete steps.

What ChatGPT Struggles With

Being honest about limitations makes you a better user:

Factual accuracy. ChatGPT can and does state incorrect things as fact. It's especially unreliable with specific numbers, dates, quotes, and citations. Always verify.

Math and precise reasoning. GPT-5.4 Thinking has sharply improved mathematical reasoning, but ChatGPT can still make errors on complex calculations. For anything where precision matters, use it to set up the problem, then verify the answer.

Real-time information. Without web search enabled, ChatGPT's knowledge has a cutoff date. It may not know about events after its training data was collected. When you need current information, make sure it's searching the web.

Consistency in long conversations. As conversations grow longer, ChatGPT may contradict earlier statements or forget constraints you set. This is a consequence of the context window limitation.

Knowing what it doesn't know. ChatGPT rarely says "I don't know." It's more likely to generate a plausible-sounding answer than admit uncertainty. Learning to recognize when it's guessing is a skill you'll develop with experience.

Personal and emotional support. ChatGPT can be empathetic, but it's not a therapist or counselor. For mental health concerns, seek professional help.

Where ChatGPT Fits in the AI Landscape

ChatGPT is the most widely used AI assistant in the world, but it's not the only one. Understanding the landscape helps you make informed choices:

- **Claude** (by Anthropic) – Known for careful, nuanced responses and strong performance on long documents. We cover Claude in depth in our companion book, *Claude: The Definitive Guide.*
- **Gemini** (by Google) – Deeply integrated with Google's ecosystem: Search, Gmail, Docs, and Android.
- **Microsoft Copilot** – Powered by OpenAI's technology, integrated into Microsoft 365 (Word, Excel, PowerPoint, Outlook).

- **Perplexity** — Focused on search and research with cited sources.

Each has its strengths. Many power users keep multiple AI assistants on hand and reach for whichever fits the task. But ChatGPT's combination of capabilities, ease of use, and enormous third-party ecosystem (custom GPTs, integrations, and developer tools) makes it the most versatile general-purpose AI assistant available today.

What You'll Learn in This Book

This book is organized to take you from your first conversation to confident, productive daily use:

- **Part I (Chapters 1–5)** gets you set up: choosing a plan, creating your account, understanding the models, and having your first conversations.
- **Part II (Chapters 6–9)** covers core skills: writing, research, everyday productivity, and professional use.
- **Part III (Chapters 10–12)** explores creative tools: image generation, video creation, and collaborative editing with Canvas.
- **Part IV (Chapters 13–23)** dives deep into every productivity feature: vision, voice, data analysis, web search, Agent Mode, Projects, custom GPTs, integrations, and more.
- **Part V (Chapters 24–26)** teaches you prompting: how to get better results, handle complex tasks, and control output formatting.
- **Part VI (Chapters 27–29)** applies ChatGPT to your world: specific guidance for students, business users, and creators.
- **Part VII (Chapters 30–32)** covers what you need to know about safety, limitations, ethics, and responsible use.
- **Part VIII (Appendices A–F)** gives you reference material: shortcuts, 75+ prompt templates, troubleshooting, a glossary, a 2026 changelog, and resources for further learning.

Every chapter is designed to be read in order or dipped into as needed. If you're new, continue with Chapter 2. If you've been using ChatGPT for a while and want to level up, skip ahead to the features you haven't explored yet.

Let's get started. Chapter 2 will help you choose the right plan for your needs.

Chapter 2: Choosing the Right Plan

Before you type your first message, one decision: which ChatGPT plan is right for you?

OpenAI offers six tiers, from completely free to enterprise-grade. The differences aren't just about price — they determine which models you can use, how many messages you can send, which features you can access, and how your data is handled.

This chapter breaks down every option so you can make an informed choice. If you're unsure, start with the Free tier. You can always upgrade later, and nothing you've done in ChatGPT is lost when you change plans.

The Plans at a Glance

Plan	Price	Best For
Free	$0/month	Trying ChatGPT, light personal use
Go	$8/month	Regular personal use on a budget
Plus	$20/month	Daily users who want full features
Pro	$200/month	Power users, researchers, professionals
Business	$25/user/month	Teams and small businesses
Enterprise	Custom pricing	Large organizations

Let's look at each one in detail.

Free

Price: $0 **What you get:** Access to GPT-5.3 Instant, ChatGPT's default model, with a cap of 10 messages every 5 hours. Once you hit that limit, you fall back to GPT-5.2 Mini for unlimited basic responses.

What you don't get: Agent Mode, Deep Research, Sora (video generation), Codex, and other advanced features. You also see ads in the United States as of May 2026.

Who it's for: The Free tier is fine if you want to try ChatGPT before committing, you use it occasionally for quick questions, or you're on a tight budget. GPT-5.3 is a capable model — even with the message limit, you can get real work done in ten messages if you're deliberate.

The honest take: The Free tier isn't a crippled demo. It's a fully functional version of ChatGPT with the same core model paying users get. The limitations are about volume and advanced features, not quality. If you're new to ChatGPT, start here. You'll know quickly whether you want more.

How to make the most of 10 messages: Ten sounds limiting, but you can stretch them. Be deliberate: instead of opening with "Hi, can you help me with something?", put your full request in the first prompt. Include all the context upfront. You can get a complete blog outline, a meal plan, or a detailed explanation in a single well-crafted message. Save follow-ups for refinements, not for clarifications you could have included upfront. Treat each message as a turn, and make each one count.

Go

Price: $8/month **What you get:** Unlimited messages with GPT-5.2 Instant, plus GPT-5.3 with up to 160 messages every 3 hours. That's a significant step up from the Free tier's 10 messages every 5 hours.

What you don't get: GPT-5.4 Thinking (the frontier reasoning model), Agent Mode, Deep Research, Sora, and Codex. Like the Free tier, Go still shows ads.

Who it's for: Go is for people who use ChatGPT regularly but don't need the most advanced features. If you're writing emails, brainstorming ideas, getting help with everyday tasks, and occasionally hitting the Free tier's message limits, Go solves the problem at a reasonable price.

The honest take: Go launched globally in January 2026 after starting as a regional plan in India. It fills an important gap — not everyone needs (or can justify) $20/month, and Go is far more generous than the Free tier. What you give up compared to Plus is access to the frontier models and advanced tools. For many people, that's a fine trade-off.

Who should skip Go and go straight to Plus? If you already know you want to generate images, use Agent Mode, or run Deep Research, Go won't get you there — those features are Plus-only. Go is best for people whose primary use is conversation: asking questions, writing drafts, brainstorming, getting advice. If that's 90% of what you do with ChatGPT, Go delivers excellent value at a price that's easier to justify than Plus.

Plus

Price: $20/month (monthly billing only — no annual discount) **What you get:** This is where ChatGPT opens up. Plus includes:

- GPT-5.3 with significantly higher message limits
- GPT-5.4 Thinking with up to 3,000 messages per week
- Agent Mode — ChatGPT can complete tasks on your behalf
- Deep Research — multi-step, cited research reports
- DALL-E image generation
- Sora video generation
- Canvas for collaborative editing
- Advanced Voice Mode
- Projects for organizing your work
- Custom GPTs (create and use)
- Web search with citations
- File uploads and data analysis
- No ads

Who it's for: Plus is the right plan for most serious users. If you use ChatGPT daily for work, school, or personal productivity, and you want access to the full feature set, this is the plan to get.

The honest take: Plus is ChatGPT's most popular paid plan, and for good reason. The jump from Go to Plus isn't just about a better model — it unlocks an entirely different category of capabilities. Agent Mode alone can save you hours of tedious work. Deep Research can replace what used to take a junior analyst half a day. The 3,000-message weekly limit on GPT-5.4 Thinking is generous enough for heavy daily use. If you can afford $20/month and you use ChatGPT regularly, Plus pays for itself.

A concrete example of the Plus difference: Say you're preparing for a job interview. On Go, you can ask ChatGPT for common interview questions and get good answers. On Plus, you can upload the job description, ask Deep Research to analyze the company's recent news and culture, have GPT-5.4 Thinking build a tailored preparation strategy, use Agent Mode to browse the company's careers page for insights, then run a mock interview with Advanced Voice Mode. Same task, different depth.

The one catch: Plus is monthly only at $20/month — no annual discount. If you use ChatGPT heavily for a few weeks and then barely at all for a month, you might prefer to subscribe and cancel as needed rather than pay year-round. There's no penalty for canceling and resubscribing — your conversations and data persist.

Pro

Price: $200/month **What you get:** Everything in Plus, with the limits removed:

- Unlimited messages across all models
- GPT-5.4 Pro — an exclusive model that dedicates significantly more compute to each query, producing higher-quality responses on complex reasoning tasks
- Extended Deep Research with longer, more thorough reports
- Priority access during peak usage
- Higher limits on Sora, Agent Mode, and other advanced features

Who it's for: Pro is for professionals whose work depends heavily on AI: researchers, consultants, developers, writers, analysts, and anyone constantly hitting Plus limits or needing the absolute best quality on complex tasks.

The honest take: Pro is expensive, and it should be. At $200/month, you need clear, measurable value from ChatGPT to justify it. The key question is whether you regularly work on problems complex enough to benefit from GPT-5.4 Pro's additional compute. If you're a researcher synthesizing dozens of papers, a developer working on complex codebases, or a consultant producing detailed analyses, Pro pays for itself quickly. If you're mostly writing emails and brainstorming, Plus is more than enough.

How to tell if Pro is worth it for you: Use Plus for a month and pay attention to three things: how often you hit message limits, how often you wish the response were better on hard problems, and how often you need extended Deep Research. If you're bumping into those ceilings weekly, Pro removes the friction. If you rarely hit limits and Plus is almost always good enough, save your $180/month. A useful heuristic: if ChatGPT saves you more than two hours per week on work you'd bill at $100+/hour, Pro pays for itself in the first week.

Business

Price: $25/user/month (monthly or annual billing) **What you get:** Everything in Plus, with team-oriented features:

- Shared team workspaces
- Admin console for managing users and permissions
- Data excluded from training by default (your company's information stays private)
- Higher message limits than individual Plus
- Centralized billing
- Priority support

Who it's for: Small to medium businesses that want to give their team access to ChatGPT with proper data controls and centralized management.

The honest take: Business solves a real problem. Many companies are uncomfortable with employees using personal ChatGPT accounts for work — and for good reason. Business gives you data privacy guarantees, the ability to manage who has access, and a single bill instead of expense reports from every team member. The per-user cost is only $5 more than Plus, and you get meaningful upgrades in both features and governance. If your company is paying for three or more Plus accounts, switching to Business is a no-brainer.

Enterprise

Price: Custom (contact OpenAI sales) **What you get:** Everything in Business, plus:

- Single sign-on (SSO) and domain verification

- Advanced security and compliance features
- MCP (Model Context Protocol) connectors for enterprise tools (Salesforce, Amplitude, Stripe, and more)
- Custom data retention policies
- Dedicated account management
- Analytics and usage dashboards
- Unlimited access to all models and features

Who it's for: Large organizations with hundreds or thousands of users, strict compliance requirements, and the need for deep integration with existing enterprise systems.

The honest take: If you're evaluating Enterprise, you're probably not making this decision alone — it's an IT and procurement discussion. The key differentiators over Business are SSO, compliance certifications, enterprise connectors, and the ability to customize data handling policies. Those matter enormously for regulated industries (healthcare, finance, legal) and large organizations with strict IT governance.

How to Decide

If you're still not sure which plan is right for you, ask yourself these questions:

How often will I use ChatGPT? - A few times a week → Free or Go - Daily → Plus - All day, every day → Plus or Pro

Do I need advanced features (Agent Mode, Deep Research, Sora)? - No → Free or Go - Yes → Plus or Pro

Am I using ChatGPT for work? - Personal use only → Any individual plan - Professional use, solo → Plus or Pro - Team use → Business - Organization-wide → Enterprise

How complex are my tasks? - Simple questions, writing help, brainstorming → Free, Go, or Plus - Complex research, advanced coding, detailed analysis → Plus or Pro - Mission-critical work requiring the best possible output → Pro

Does data privacy matter for my use case? - Using for personal tasks → Any plan - Using with sensitive business information → Business or Enterprise

A Note on Pricing Changes

AI pricing is evolving fast. OpenAI has adjusted plans and pricing multiple times since ChatGPT launched, and they'll likely continue. The prices here are accurate as of May 2026, but check chatgpt.com/pricing for the latest before deciding.

The trend has been more capability at each price point over time. Features that were once Pro-only tend to trickle down to Plus, and Plus features eventually reach Go and Free. If a feature you want is currently above your budget, it may become available at your tier in the coming months.

Student and Education Access

If you're a student, two programs are worth knowing about:

ChatGPT Edu: Some universities provide ChatGPT access to students and faculty through this institutional offering — similar to Enterprise but built for academic institutions. Check with your school's IT department.

Codex for Students: Verified university students in the United States and Canada can receive $100 in credits for Codex, OpenAI's agentic coding tool. If you're studying computer science or any field that involves programming, claim it.

What Happens When You Upgrade or Downgrade

Upgrading is instant. The moment your payment processes, you get access to the new tier's features and limits. Your existing conversations, memories, custom GPTs, and Projects are preserved.

Downgrading takes effect at the end of your current billing period. You don't lose your conversations or data, but you'll lose access to features not included in the new tier. For example, if you downgrade from Plus to Go, conversations you created with Agent Mode are still visible, but you won't be able to start new agent tasks.

You're never locked in. No contracts, no cancellation fees, no long-term commitments on any individual plan.

Now that you've chosen a plan (or decided to start with Free), let's get your account set up. Chapter 3 walks you through every step.

Chapter 3: Setting Up Your Account

Getting started with ChatGPT takes about two minutes. This chapter walks you through creating your account, navigating the interface on every platform, and configuring the settings that matter most — including the privacy controls worth reviewing before your first real conversation.

Creating Your Account

Go to **chat.com** (yes, OpenAI owns that domain — it redirects to chatgpt.com). You'll see the ChatGPT interface with a prompt to sign up or log in.

Click **Sign up** and choose one of four methods:

- **Email address** — Enter your email, create a password, and verify via a confirmation link
- **Google account** — One-click sign-in with your Google credentials
- **Apple account** — Sign in with your Apple ID (supports Hide My Email)
- **Microsoft account** — Sign in with your Microsoft/Outlook credentials

Any method works equally well. If you already use one of these accounts for other services, choosing it means one less password to remember. If you'd rather keep your ChatGPT account separate, use a dedicated email address.

A practical tip on account choice: If you plan to use ChatGPT for work, choose your email carefully. ChatGPT accounts can't be transferred between email addresses easily. If you sign up with a personal Gmail and later want to use ChatGPT for work on a Business plan, you may need to create a separate account with your work email. Some people keep two accounts — one personal, one professional — especially if their employer has different data handling requirements. That said, if you're just getting started, don't overthink it. Pick whatever gets you in the door fastest.

After signing in, you'll be asked for your name and date of birth. OpenAI requires users to be at least 13 (18 in some regions). That's it — you're in.

The Interface: Web

The web interface at chat.com is where most people use ChatGPT. Here's what you're looking at:

The sidebar (left) contains: - Your conversation history, organized by date - Projects — folders for organizing related conversations - A search bar to find past conversations - The option to start a new chat

The main area (center) is where conversations happen: - The message input bar at the bottom, where you type your prompts - The + button to attach files, images, or start a conversation with specific tools - The microphone button for voice input - The voice mode button for full voice conversation - A model selector (if you're on a paid plan) showing which model is active

The top bar shows: - The current model name - Access to your account settings (profile icon)

Starting a conversation is as simple as typing in the message bar and pressing Enter (or clicking the send button). That's all there is to it. ChatGPT responds, and you continue by typing follow-up messages.

A few things that trip up new users: The model selector at the top might show "GPT-5.3" or "GPT-5.4" depending on your plan. If you don't see a selector, you're on the Free plan using the default model — that's fine. The search bar in the sidebar searches your past conversations, not the web. And the sidebar fills up quickly — ChatGPT names each conversation automatically based on its content, which makes finding things later easier than you'd expect.

The Interface: Mobile Apps

ChatGPT is available as a native app on both **iOS** (iPhone and iPad) and **Android**. The apps are free to download from the App Store and Google Play, respectively.

The mobile interface mirrors the web version with a few differences:

- **Voice mode is front and center.** The voice button sits prominently, making spoken conversations easy. This is where Advanced Voice Mode shines — it feels like talking to a knowledgeable friend.

- **Camera access.** You can take photos directly within the app and share them with ChatGPT for analysis. Point your phone at a restaurant menu, a math problem, a plant you want to identify, or an error message on your screen.
- **Haptics and notifications.** The app can notify you when scheduled tasks complete or Agent Mode finishes a task.
- **Widgets.** On both iOS and Android, you can add a ChatGPT widget to your home screen for quick access.

The mobile apps use the same account as the web version. Conversations, memories, and settings sync across all devices automatically.

The Interface: Desktop Apps

ChatGPT has dedicated desktop apps for both **macOS** and **Windows**.

The desktop apps offer everything the web version does, plus:

- **System-wide access.** On Mac, invoke ChatGPT with a keyboard shortcut from any application. On Windows, use Alt+Space (or customize the shortcut in Settings).
- **Screenshot sharing.** Capture and share your screen with ChatGPT without leaving the app you're working in.
- **Voice mode.** Full voice conversations work on the Windows desktop app. Advanced Voice Mode was removed from the macOS desktop app in January 2026 — for voice conversations on Mac, use chat.com in your browser.

If you use ChatGPT throughout your workday, the desktop app is worth installing. Having it a keyboard shortcut away, rather than a browser tab you have to hunt for, makes a meaningful difference in how often and how naturally you reach for it.

The screenshot feature deserves special mention. On both Mac and Windows, you can capture part of your screen and share it with ChatGPT. This is useful for error messages, a UI you're confused by, or feedback on a design you're working on. Instead of describing what you're seeing ("I have this error that says something about a null reference..."), screenshot it and ask "What does this mean?" The quality of ChatGPT's help jumps when it can see exactly what you're looking at.

Your First Settings Check

Before you start using ChatGPT in earnest, take five minutes to review your settings. Click your profile icon in the top-right corner, then select **Settings**.

Memory

ChatGPT can remember information across conversations — your name, your job, your preferences, your ongoing projects. This is called *Memory*, and it's on by default.

What to know: - Memory makes ChatGPT more useful over time. It won't ask the same questions repeatedly. - You can view everything ChatGPT has remembered at **Settings → Personalization → Memory**. - You can delete individual memories or clear all of them at any time. - For a conversation that doesn't create memories, use **Temporary Chat** (more on this below).

Our recommendation: Leave Memory on. It meaningfully improves your experience. Review your stored memories periodically and delete anything you don't want retained.

Custom Instructions

Custom Instructions let you give ChatGPT standing directions that apply to every conversation. It's one of the most powerful and underused features.

You can set two things:

1. **What would you like ChatGPT to know about you?** — Your role, expertise, preferences, and context. For example: "I'm a marketing manager at a mid-size B2B software company. I manage a team of five. I prefer concise, actionable responses."
2. **How would you like ChatGPT to respond?** — Your preferred format, tone, and style. For example: "Use bullet points when listing options. Avoid corporate jargon. Be direct — don't pad responses with unnecessary qualifiers."

Our recommendation: Fill these in now, even if you revise them later. ChatGPT with Custom Instructions tuned to your needs is dramatically more useful than generic ChatGPT. We cover advanced Custom Instructions strategies in Chapter 22.

A quick starter example: If you're not sure what to put in Custom Instructions, start simple. In "About You": *"I'm a [your role] at a [type of company]. I prefer practical, actionable advice."* In "How to respond": *"Be concise. Use bullet points when listing options. Don't open with pleasantries — get to the answer."* That alone noticeably improves the experience. Refine later as you discover what you like and don't like about ChatGPT's default behavior.

Data Controls

This is the section most people skip and shouldn't. Go to **Settings → Data Controls**.

Improve the model for everyone: Controls whether your conversations can be used to train future versions of ChatGPT's models. Turn it off and your conversations are still processed to generate responses, but they won't be used for training.

- **For personal, non-sensitive tasks**, leaving this on is fine and helps improve the product.
- **For work or any sensitive information**, turn it off. This is especially important if your company doesn't have a ChatGPT usage policy yet.
- **Business and Enterprise plans** have this off by default — your data is never used for training.

Chat history: You can turn off chat history entirely. When it's off, new conversations won't appear in your sidebar and won't be used for training. OpenAI still retains conversations for 30 days for safety monitoring before permanently deleting them.

Export your data: You can request a full export of your ChatGPT data at any time, delivered as a downloadable file containing all your conversations. Worth doing periodically if you use ChatGPT for important work — think of it as a backup of your AI conversation history.

Delete your account: If you ever want to leave entirely, you can delete your account and all associated data from this screen.

Our recommendation on data controls: If you're using ChatGPT for anything beyond casual personal questions, turn off "Improve the model for everyone." Response quality doesn't change — the toggle only affects whether your conversations are used for training future models. The peace of mind is worth the click. You can always turn it back on later.

Temporary Chat

Temporary Chat is a per-conversation privacy mode. When you start a Temporary Chat:

- The conversation won't appear in your history
- It won't create or access memories
- It won't be used for model training

Think of it as incognito mode for ChatGPT. Use it when you're asking about something you'd rather not have in your conversation history, or when you're helping someone else with their question on your account.

To start a Temporary Chat, click the **new chat** button and look for the Temporary Chat toggle, or select it from the model dropdown menu.

When to use Temporary Chat: Planning a surprise party and don't want it showing up when your partner borrows your laptop? Temporary Chat. Asking a sensitive health question you'd rather not have in your history? Temporary Chat. Helping a coworker debug something on your account? Temporary Chat. Simple feature, but it removes the friction of worrying about what's being stored.

Syncing Across Devices

One detail easy to overlook but useful in practice: your ChatGPT account syncs everything across all devices — web, mobile, and desktop. Conversations you start on your phone continue seamlessly on your laptop. Memories, Custom Instructions, and Projects are available everywhere. Start a long research conversation on your desktop at work, and it's right there in your sidebar when you continue on your phone during your commute.

The one exception is downloaded files. If ChatGPT generates a spreadsheet or chart on your desktop, the download link lives in that conversation — you can access the conversation from any device, but you'll need to download the file on whichever device you want it on.

Accessibility

ChatGPT supports several accessibility features:

- **Screen reader compatibility** — The web and mobile interfaces work with VoiceOver (iOS/Mac), TalkBack (Android), and other screen readers.
- **Keyboard navigation** — The web interface is fully navigable by keyboard.
- **Voice Mode** — For users who have difficulty typing, voice conversations provide a hands-free way to interact with ChatGPT. Advanced Voice Mode is particularly powerful for accessibility — a fully capable AI assistant that requires no typing at all.
- **Font size and display** — Use your browser's or device's built-in zoom and display settings; ChatGPT's interface scales accordingly.
- **High contrast and dark mode** — ChatGPT supports dark mode on all platforms, reducing eye strain in low-light environments. Toggle it in Settings or let it follow your system preferences.

You're Ready

Your account is set up, your settings are configured, and you know your way around the interface. Before we dive into your first conversations, Chapter 4 will help you understand the different AI models available to you — when to use which one, and why it matters.

Chapter 4: Choosing the Right Model

If you're on a paid plan, you've probably noticed ChatGPT lets you choose between different AI models. It can feel overwhelming at first — what's the difference, and when does it matter?

This chapter demystifies model selection. By the end, you'll know which model to use for any given task, and more importantly, when you can stop thinking about it entirely.

The Current Model Lineup

As of May 2026, ChatGPT runs on the GPT-5 family of models. Here are the ones you'll encounter:

GPT-5.3 Instant — The Everyday Default

This is the model most people use most of the time, and for good reason. GPT-5.3 Instant is:

- **Fast.** Responses come back in seconds.
- **Capable.** It handles writing, research, brainstorming, coding, and analysis at a high level.
- **Auto-switching.** GPT-5.3 includes a single auto-switching system that routes your request to the right capability — standard conversation, web search, code execution, or image generation. You don't pick the tool; the model picks it.

GPT-5.3 Instant is available on Free (with limits), Go (with generous limits), and Plus/Pro (with high limits).

When to use it: For the vast majority of your ChatGPT interactions. Writing emails, answering questions, summarizing documents, generating ideas, having conversations, creating images — GPT-5.3 handles all of these well.

Try it yourself: Ask GPT-5.3 to write a professional email declining a meeting invitation. Then ask it to explain how compound interest works. Then ask it to brainstorm ten names for a history podcast. The responses are fast, useful, and need no model selection on your part. That's the point — GPT-5.3 is the workhorse you'll use for 80% of everything.

GPT-5.4 Thinking — The Frontier Reasoning Model

GPT-5.4 is OpenAI's most capable model. The clue is in the name: *Thinking*. The model takes more time to reason through problems before responding. You'll sometimes see a brief "thinking" indicator before the response begins.

GPT-5.4 Thinking excels at:

- **Complex reasoning.** Multi-step logic problems, mathematical proofs, scientific analysis.
- **Advanced coding.** Architecting systems, debugging subtle issues, writing production-quality code.
- **Document understanding.** Analyzing long, complex documents — contracts, research papers, financial reports.
- **Spreadsheet and data work.** Creating and editing spreadsheets, building charts, data transformation.
- **Agentic workflows.** When ChatGPT needs to plan and execute multi-step tasks, GPT-5.4 is the engine behind it.
- **Polished output.** Presentations, frontend code, and any task where the quality of the final product matters.

GPT-5.4 Thinking is available on Plus (up to 3,000 messages/week) and Pro (unlimited).

When to use it: When the task is complex. If you're asking ChatGPT to do something that requires careful reasoning — analyzing a business problem, working through a technical challenge, producing something polished and precise — switch to GPT-5.4.

A real example of the difference: Ask both models to solve this: "A store is running a promotion where you buy 3 items, the cheapest is free. You have items priced at $15, $22, $8, $30, and $12. What's the optimal way to group them to minimize your total cost?" GPT-5.3 often gives a quick answer that may or may not account for the optimal grouping. GPT-5.4 methodically works through the combinations and finds the true minimum. On a question like this, the "thinking" time pays off.

What the "thinking" indicator looks like: When GPT-5.4 is working on a hard problem, you'll see a brief "Thinking..." indicator before the response appears. It can last anywhere from a few seconds to thirty seconds or more. Don't interrupt it — this is when the model is doing its best work. The pause is the feature.

GPT-5.4 Pro — Maximum Compute

Available exclusively to Pro subscribers ($200/month), GPT-5.4 Pro dedicates more computational resources to each query. It's not a different model — it's the same GPT-5.4 architecture with more "thinking time" allocated to your request.

When to use it: For the hardest problems you encounter. Complex research synthesis, difficult mathematical reasoning, and high-stakes professional work where you want the absolute best output ChatGPT can produce. If you're on Pro, use it when the quality ceiling matters more than response speed.

The honest take on GPT-5.4 Pro: On everyday tasks, you won't notice a difference between GPT-5.4 and GPT-5.4 Pro. The gap appears only on the hardest problems — the kind where GPT-5.4 gives a good answer but Pro gives a noticeably better one. Think: analyzing a complex legal contract with nested conditional clauses, or synthesizing conflicting research findings into a coherent framework. If you're on Pro and wondering when to use it, ask yourself: "Would I spend an hour on this myself to get it right?" If yes, Pro is worth the extra compute time.

GPT-5.2 Mini and GPT-5.2 Instant

These are the lighter models in the lineup:

- **GPT-5.2 Mini** is what Free users fall back to after hitting their GPT-5.3 message limit. Less capable but still functional for basic questions and simple tasks.
- **GPT-5.2 Instant** is the unlimited model available to Go subscribers. Faster than GPT-5.3 but less capable on complex tasks.

You won't usually choose these manually — they're what the system provides when your primary model's limits are reached.

The Practical Guide to Model Selection

Here's a simple framework:

Task	Model	Why
Quick questions	GPT-5.3	Fast, good enough
Writing emails	GPT-5.3	Speed matters more than peak quality
Brainstorming	GPT-5.3	Volume of ideas matters more than depth
Casual conversation	GPT-5.3	No need for heavy reasoning
Summarizing a document	GPT-5.3	Handles this well
Generating images	GPT-5.3	Auto-routes to DALL-E
Complex math or logic	GPT-5.4	Reasoning model catches errors GPT-5.3 misses
Analyzing a contract	GPT-5.4	Document understanding is significantly better
Writing production code	GPT-5.4	Produces cleaner, more correct code
Research report	GPT-5.4	Better at synthesis and nuance
Creating a presentation	GPT-5.4	Polished output quality
Agent Mode tasks	GPT-5.4	Powers agentic workflows by default
Hardest problems	GPT-5.4 Pro	Maximum compute for maximum quality

When Model Selection Doesn't Matter

Here's something most guides won't tell you: **for many common tasks, the model you choose barely matters.**

If you're asking ChatGPT to write a grocery list, draft a casual email, translate a sentence, or explain a basic concept, GPT-5.3 and GPT-5.4 produce nearly identical results. The differences show up on harder tasks — the kind that need careful reasoning, nuanced judgment, or precise technical output.

A good rule of thumb: **start with GPT-5.3. If the response isn't good enough, try GPT-5.4.** You'll quickly develop an intuition for which tasks benefit from the more powerful model.

Here's how that intuition develops in practice. After a few weeks, most users settle into a pattern: GPT-5.3 for conversations, emails, brainstorming, and casual questions. They switch to GPT-5.4 when they upload a complex document, need to debug code, want a polished piece of writing, or are working through a problem that needs careful step-by-step reasoning. The switch becomes second nature — like knowing when to reach for a calculator versus doing math in your head.

Auto-Switching: Let ChatGPT Decide

One of the most useful changes in the GPT-5.3 era is auto-switching. Instead of manually selecting tools (web search, code interpreter, DALL-E), the model determines what you need based on your message.

Ask about today's news? It searches the web. Upload a CSV? It opens the code interpreter. Ask for an image? It invokes DALL-E. No toggles — just describe what you want.

You spend less time thinking about which model or tool to use and more time thinking about what you want to accomplish. The AI handles the routing.

Legacy Models

If you've been using ChatGPT for a while, you may remember models like GPT-4, GPT-4o, o1, and o3. These are no longer available in ChatGPT — the GPT-5 family has superseded them. When you see references to those older models online or in other guides, GPT-5.3 replaces GPT-4o for everyday use, and GPT-5.4 replaces o1/o3 for reasoning tasks.

The progression has been toward fewer, more capable models instead of a confusing menu of specialized options. That's a good thing for users.

Why legacy model names still matter: You'll see references to GPT-4, GPT-4o, o1, o3-mini, and other older names in online tutorials, YouTube videos, and blog posts. Most of the prompting advice written for those models still works with the GPT-5 family — the fundamental approach to getting good results hasn't changed. But specific capability claims ("GPT-4 can't do X") may no longer hold. When reading older guides, focus on the techniques and ignore the model-specific limitations — the GPT-5 family has resolved many of the issues people wrote about.

Understanding Message Limits

Each plan has limits on how many messages you can send with each model within a given time period. These limits reset on a rolling basis:

- **Free:** 10 GPT-5.3 messages every 5 hours, then unlimited GPT-5.2 Mini
- **Go:** 160 GPT-5.3 messages every 3 hours, unlimited GPT-5.2 Instant
- **Plus:** Higher GPT-5.3 limits, 3,000 GPT-5.4 messages per week
- **Pro:** Unlimited across all models

When you're approaching a limit, ChatGPT lets you know. If you hit it, you can either wait for the limit to reset or use the fallback model.

Practical tip: If you're on Plus and doing a mix of simple and complex work throughout the day, use GPT-5.3 for the simple stuff. Save GPT-5.4 messages for tasks that actually benefit from the extra reasoning power. At 3,000 messages per week, that's over 400 per day — generous for most users, but worth being strategic about if you're a very heavy user.

What happens when you hit a limit: ChatGPT gives you a clear warning as you approach your cap. If you hit it, you're not locked out — you fall back to a less powerful model. On Plus, if you exhaust your GPT-5.4 messages for the week, you can still use GPT-5.3 without restriction. On Free, once your 10 GPT-5.3 messages are used in a 5-hour window, you drop to GPT-5.2 Mini. The experience is seamless — you don't lose your conversation or get an error. The responses just come from a different model until your limit resets.

An edge case worth knowing: Long conversations with many messages consume your limit faster than you'd expect, because each message in the thread counts. If you're doing intensive work on GPT-5.4, start a new conversation for each distinct task rather than running everything in a single mega-thread. That also tends to produce better responses, since each new conversation starts with fresh context.

The Bottom Line

Don't overthink model selection. The simplest possible advice:

1. **Use GPT-5.3 for everything by default.** Fast, capable, handles the vast majority of tasks well.
2. **Switch to GPT-5.4 when the task is hard.** Complex reasoning, precise analysis, polished output, or when GPT-5.3's response wasn't good enough.
3. **Use GPT-5.4 Pro if you have it and the stakes are high.** Research, professional deliverables, and problems where you need the ceiling, not the floor.
4. **Let auto-switching handle tool selection.** Describe what you want. The model figures out whether to search, run code, generate an image, or just talk.

With that understood, you're ready for the fun part. Chapter 5 is about having your first real conversations with ChatGPT — and learning the basics of how to talk to it effectively.

Chapter 5: Your First Conversations

You've set up your account, chosen your plan, and understand the models. Now it's time to actually use ChatGPT. This chapter covers the fundamentals of a productive conversation — from your first message to the instincts that separate casual users from effective ones.

Just Talk to It

The most important thing to understand about ChatGPT is that you don't need special syntax, keywords, or commands. Write like you're talking to a smart, helpful colleague.

If you want to know how to cook risotto, type: *"How do I make risotto?"*

If you want help with an email, type: *"Help me write an email to my landlord asking for a lease renewal at the same rate."*

If you want to understand something, type: *"Explain how mortgages work. I'm a first-time homebuyer and I don't know where to start."*

That's it. No tricks, no special formatting. ChatGPT is designed to understand natural language, including imperfect grammar, typos, and incomplete thoughts. You don't need to write perfectly — just communicate what you want.

This is worth emphasizing because many people approach ChatGPT like a search query — stripping out articles, using keywords, trying to speak "robot." You don't need to. The more naturally you write, the better the results tend to be. *"What's a good restaurant in Denver for date night, something with a nice atmosphere but not crazy expensive?"* works beautifully. You're having a conversation, not constructing a database query.

Your First Ten Prompts

If you're staring at an empty chat and not sure where to begin, try these. Each one demonstrates a different capability:

1. **Ask a question:** *"What's the difference between a Roth IRA and a traditional IRA?"*

2. **Get an explanation:** *"Explain the greenhouse effect like I'm twelve years old."*
3. **Write something:** *"Write a professional but warm thank-you email to a colleague who helped me with a presentation."*
4. **Brainstorm:** *"Give me ten creative names for a dog grooming business."*
5. **Summarize:** *"Summarize the main arguments for and against remote work in three bullet points each."*
6. **Translate:** *"How do you say 'Where is the nearest pharmacy?' in Japanese, Spanish, and French?"*
7. **Plan:** *"I have friends visiting for the weekend. Plan a Saturday in [your city] including breakfast, an activity, lunch, and dinner."*
8. **Analyze:** *"What are the pros and cons of leasing vs. buying a car?"*
9. **Create:** *"Write a short bedtime story about a cat who becomes an astronaut."*
10. **Advise:** *"I'm nervous about a job interview tomorrow for a product manager role. What should I prepare for?"*

Try all ten. Notice how different the responses are — from factual explanations to creative writing to practical advice. That range is what makes ChatGPT useful across so many areas of life.

The Art of the Follow-Up

Your first message starts a conversation. The follow-ups are where the real power is.

ChatGPT remembers everything you've said in the current conversation, so you can refine, redirect, and build on its responses:

- **Make it shorter:** *"That's good but too long. Give me a version that's half the length."*
- **Change the tone:** *"Can you make that more casual? It sounds too corporate."*

- **Go deeper:** *"Tell me more about the third point."*
- **Redirect:** *"Actually, let's focus on the budget aspect instead."*
- **Challenge it:** *"I'm not sure that's right. Can you double-check?"*
- **Get alternatives:** *"Give me three more options."*

Think of it like editing with a collaborator. Your first prompt gets a draft. Your follow-ups shape it into what you need. The best ChatGPT users rarely accept the first response as-is — they iterate.

Here's how follow-ups transform output. Say you ask ChatGPT to write a thank-you note to a colleague. The first draft is polished but generic. You reply: *"Make it warmer — mention specifically that she stayed late to help with the client presentation."* Now it's personal. You reply again: *"Shorter. Three sentences max."* Now it's the right length. Two follow-ups, twenty seconds, and the output went from "fine" to "exactly what I wanted." That's the rhythm of effective ChatGPT use.

Be Specific

The single biggest factor in getting good responses from ChatGPT is specificity. Compare these two prompts:

Vague: *"Help me with my resume."* ChatGPT doesn't know what kind of help you need, what industry you're in, what role you're targeting, or what's wrong with your current resume. You'll get generic advice.

Specific: *"I'm a software engineer with 5 years of experience applying for senior roles at mid-size startups. Here's my current resume [paste it]. The main feedback I've gotten is that it doesn't highlight leadership. Can you suggest revisions to the experience section that emphasize team leadership and mentoring?"*

The second prompt gives ChatGPT everything it needs to give you a useful response: your background, your goal, your current material, the specific problem, and the section to focus on.

You don't need this much detail for every question. *"What's the capital of France?"* doesn't need context. But for any task where response quality matters, more context produces better output. A useful framework:

- **Who are you?** (Your role, expertise level, situation)
- **What do you want?** (The specific output you need)
- **Why?** (The context or purpose)
- **How?** (Format, length, tone preferences)

Give It a Role

One of the most effective techniques — even for beginners — is telling ChatGPT who to be:

- *"You are an experienced hiring manager at a tech company. Review my resume and tell me what would make you put it in the 'yes' pile."*
- *"You are a patient math tutor. Walk me through this problem step by step."*
- *"You are a travel agent specializing in budget European trips. Help me plan a 10-day itinerary for under $2,000."*
- *"You are a nutritionist. Create a meal plan for someone who's trying to eat more protein and less sugar."*

Giving ChatGPT a role does two things: it activates relevant knowledge, and it sets the tone and perspective for the conversation. A "patient math tutor" explains differently than a "math professor" — and both differ from the default ChatGPT voice.

Try this experiment: Ask the same question — *"What should I consider before buying my first home?"* — three times, each with a different role: a real estate agent, a financial advisor, and a home inspector. You'll get three meaningfully different responses. The real estate agent emphasizes location, market timing, and what to look for in a listing. The financial advisor focuses on mortgage options, down payment strategies, and debt-to-income ratios. The home inspector talks about red flags, inspection contingencies, and maintenance costs. All three are valuable — together, they give you a far more complete picture than a single generic response would.

When to Start a New Chat

ChatGPT conversations don't expire, and you can always come back to a previous chat and continue where you left off. But sometimes it's better to start fresh. Here's when:

Start a new chat when: - You're switching to a completely different topic - The current conversation has gotten long (dozens of messages) and responses seem to be drifting - You want to try a different approach to a problem without the baggage of previous attempts - You've given instructions in the current chat that you don't want applied to your next task

Continue the current chat when: - You're building on what you've already discussed - You've established context (your role, your project, your preferences) that would take time to re-explain - You're iterating on a specific piece of output (a document, a plan, code)

Understanding Why ChatGPT "Forgets"

If you've had a long conversation and ChatGPT seems to forget something you mentioned earlier, you've bumped into the *context window* — the maximum amount of text the model can consider at once.

Think of it as a sliding window. As the conversation grows, the window moves forward. Earlier messages eventually fall outside it and vanish from the model's working memory. When that happens:

- ChatGPT may contradict something it said earlier
- It may forget constraints or instructions you set
- It may ask you something you've already answered

It's not a bug — it's a fundamental architectural limitation. The simplest fix is to start a new conversation when things drift, restating the key context upfront. We cover advanced strategies for managing long conversations in Chapter 25.

Reading the Response

ChatGPT's responses aren't all created equal, and learning to read them critically is an important skill.

Watch for hedging language. Phrases like "it's possible that," "some people believe," or "this could vary" are signals ChatGPT is less confident. That's helpful — it's telling you the answer might not be definitive.

Watch for false confidence. Conversely, when ChatGPT states something with total certainty, it isn't necessarily correct. This is especially true for specific facts, numbers, and dates. If it says "The company was founded in 2014" without hedging, it might be right — or it might have made that up.

Watch for lists that trail off. When ChatGPT gives you a list that starts strong and gets generic toward the end, the first few items are usually its best answers. The tail is often filler.

Watch for the "echo." If you state something incorrect in your prompt and ChatGPT agrees with it, that's *sycophancy* — the model's tendency to agree with the user. Push back: *"Are you sure? I might be wrong about that."*

Practical Tips for Better Conversations

One thing at a time. If you have three separate questions, ask them in three messages rather than one. ChatGPT handles focused requests better than multi-part ones.

Show, don't tell. Instead of describing the format you want, show an example: *"Format your response like this: [example]. Now do the same for..."*

Ask it to think step by step. For complex problems, adding *"Think through this step by step"* to your prompt improves reasoning quality.

Request drafts, not finals. Frame your request as a starting point: *"Draft a first version of..."* This sets the expectation that you'll iterate, and it often produces better initial output because the model doesn't try to nail it in one shot.

Use it conversationally. The more natural you are, the better ChatGPT responds. You don't need complete, formal sentences. *"Make it punchier"* works as well as *"Please revise the above text to be more concise and impactful."*

Don't be afraid to say "no." If ChatGPT gives you something you don't want, say so: *"No, that's not what I meant. I want..."* It won't be offended. It will try again.

Copy and paste freely. One of the most underused techniques is pasting content directly into ChatGPT. Paste an email you received and ask for help drafting a reply. Paste a paragraph from a report and ask ChatGPT to simplify it. Paste a recipe and ask for substitutions. Paste an error message and ask what it means. ChatGPT works best with the actual text, not your summary of it.

Ask "what else?" After ChatGPT gives you a response, try *"What else should I know about this?"* or *"What am I not thinking about?"* These open-ended follow-ups often surface the most valuable insights — the things you didn't know to ask about.

You're Off and Running

You now know enough to have productive conversations with ChatGPT. The fundamentals are simple: be specific, iterate, give it context, and don't accept the first draft if it's not what you need.

The next four chapters dive into the core skills most people use ChatGPT for: writing, research, everyday productivity, and professional work. Each builds on what you've learned here and shows you how to get the most out of ChatGPT for your most common tasks.

Part II: Core Skills

"The real problem is not whether machines think but whether men do."

— B.F. Skinner

Chapter 6: Writing with ChatGPT

Writing is the most common reason people use ChatGPT, and it's where the tool delivers its most immediate, obvious value. Whether you're drafting a quick email or working on a ten-page report, ChatGPT can dramatically speed up your writing — not by replacing you, but by giving you a starting point, a second opinion, or a fresh perspective.

This chapter covers the major categories of writing you can do with ChatGPT and the techniques that produce the best results.

The Writer's Workflow

The most effective way to use ChatGPT for writing isn't to ask for a finished piece and copy-paste it. Treat it as a writing partner in a multi-step process:

1. **Brief it.** Tell ChatGPT what you need: the type of writing, the audience, the purpose, the tone, and any constraints (length, format, key points to include).
2. **Get a first draft.** Let ChatGPT produce something. Don't expect perfection.
3. **Iterate.** Give feedback: "make it shorter," "more formal," "add an example here," "the second paragraph is weak."
4. **Polish.** Make your own edits. Add your voice, your specific knowledge, your personal touches.

This workflow beats a single prompt, and it beats writing from scratch. You get ChatGPT's speed and breadth combined with your judgment and authenticity.

Emails and Messages

Email is where ChatGPT earns its keep fastest. Most people write dozens of emails a week, and most of those emails follow predictable patterns.

Simple request: *"Write a short email to my team letting them know we're moving our weekly standup from Tuesday to Wednesday starting next week."*

With tone guidance: *"Write a polite but firm email to a vendor who delivered the wrong order. I want a replacement, not a refund. Keep it professional — we want to maintain the relationship."*

Reply assistance: *"Here's an email I received [paste email]. Draft a reply that accepts the meeting but proposes Thursday instead of Friday."*

The key to great email prompts: - Specify the recipient and your relationship to them - State the purpose clearly - Indicate the tone: formal, casual, friendly, firm, apologetic - Mention anything that should or shouldn't be included - Specify length if it matters ("keep it under five sentences")

ChatGPT is especially useful for emails you've been procrastinating on — the difficult ones where you're not sure how to say what you need to say. Give it the situation, tell it your goal, let it draft something. Revising its draft is almost always easier than staring at a blank compose window.

A prompt for the hardest emails: *"I need to email my manager about a mistake I made on the Johnson account. I accidentally sent the invoice to the wrong contact, and the client called to complain. I've already fixed it. I need to own the mistake, explain what happened, describe what I've done to fix it, and explain what I'll do to prevent it in the future. Tone: professional, accountable, not groveling."*

The prompt includes the full situation, not just "help me write an email." The more context you give about the emotional dynamics — who's involved, what went wrong, what the relationship is like — the better the draft. ChatGPT is especially good at finding the right tone for delicate communications where you know what you need to say but not how to say it.

Batch email writing: If you have several emails to write, ChatGPT can knock them out quickly. Try: *"I need to write three emails. First, a follow-up to a client who hasn't responded in two weeks. Second, a thank-you to a vendor who expedited our order. Third, a request to my team to submit their hours by Friday. All should be professional, friendly, and under five sentences."* You'll get all three in one response.

Blog Posts and Articles

ChatGPT can help with every stage of article writing:

Brainstorming topics: *"I run a personal finance blog for millennials. Give me 15 article ideas for this month."*

Creating outlines: *"Create a detailed outline for a 1,500-word article about how to negotiate a salary raise. Include an introduction, 4-5 main sections, and a conclusion."*

Writing drafts: *"Using this outline, write the full article. Tone should be encouraging but practical. Use real-world examples."*

Improving existing writing: *"Here's my draft [paste text]. Improve the flow between paragraphs, tighten the language, and make the conclusion more compelling."*

Important: If you're publishing content under your name, rewrite ChatGPT's output in your own voice. AI-generated text has a recognizable style — slightly formal, heavy on parallel structure, fond of phrases like "it's important to note" and "in today's fast-paced world." Your readers follow you for your voice, not ChatGPT's.

A technique for maintaining your voice: Instead of asking ChatGPT to write the article and then rewriting it, give it examples of your previous writing first. *"Here are two paragraphs from my blog that represent my writing style [paste text]. Now write the introduction to a new article about negotiating freelance rates, matching this style."* ChatGPT is good at mimicking a style when given examples. It won't be perfect — you'll still need to edit — but the output starts much closer to your voice.

The outline-first approach: For longer articles, many writers find that asking ChatGPT for an outline, approving or modifying it, then writing the article themselves (with ChatGPT filling in sections as needed) produces better results than having ChatGPT write the whole draft. You keep creative control over structure and flow while using ChatGPT as a writing accelerator for individual sections.

Social Media Content

ChatGPT is excellent at generating social media posts, especially when you give it context about your brand and audience:

"Write five LinkedIn posts about the importance of mentorship in tech. I'm a senior engineering manager. Tone should be reflective and authentic, not corporate. Each post should be 150-200 words."

"Write a Twitter/X thread (7 tweets) breaking down the basics of compound interest for people in their twenties. Make it engaging and use simple language."

"Create three Instagram caption options for a photo of our team at a company retreat. We're a small startup — keep it fun and genuine."

Tips for social media prompts: - Specify the platform (each has different norms) - Include your brand voice or personal style - Ask for multiple options — you'll rarely love the first one - Request hashtag suggestions if applicable - Give it examples of posts you've liked

Editing and Proofreading

Sometimes you don't need ChatGPT to write — you need it to improve what you've already written.

Proofreading: *"Proofread the following text for grammar, spelling, and punctuation errors. Don't change the style or tone, just fix mistakes: [paste text]"*

Editing for clarity: *"Edit this paragraph for clarity. The ideas are right but the writing is clunky: [paste text]"*

Tone adjustment: *"Rewrite this email to be more diplomatic. The current version sounds accusatory: [paste text]"*

Simplification: *"Rewrite this for a general audience. Remove jargon and make it accessible to someone with no technical background: [paste text]"*

Tightening: *"Cut this down to half the length without losing any key points: [paste text]"*

When editing, be specific about what to change and what to preserve. "Edit this" is vague. "Fix the grammar but keep my conversational tone" is actionable.

The "track changes" approach: If you want to see exactly what ChatGPT changed, try this: *"Edit this text for clarity. Show me only the sentences you changed, with the original on one line and your revision on the next."* That gives you a diff-like view, so you can accept or reject individual changes rather than compare two full blocks of text.

Caveat about editing: ChatGPT sometimes "improves" things that didn't need improving. Ask it to proofread and it may rephrase sentences that were already fine. Be specific: *"Only fix actual errors — grammar, spelling, and punctuation. Don't rephrase anything that's already correct."* The more precisely you define the scope, the less you'll have to undo.

Translation

ChatGPT handles translation with impressive fluency across dozens of languages. It's especially good at:

- **Conversational translation:** Not just word-for-word, but natural-sounding translations that capture idioms and cultural nuances
- **Formal vs. informal registers:** It understands the difference between formal and casual speech in languages that make that distinction (French tu/vous, Japanese keigo, German du/Sie)
- **Contextual translation:** Give it the context of the communication and it'll choose the right phrasing

"Translate this business email into formal Brazilian Portuguese: [paste text]"

"How would a local say 'Can you recommend a good restaurant near here?' in casual Italian?"

Caveat: For high-stakes translations (legal documents, medical information, official communications), have a professional translator review ChatGPT's output. It's good, but it can miss subtle meanings that matter.

A useful translation trick: If you're writing something that will be translated, ask ChatGPT to write with translation in mind: *"Write this product description using simple, clear sentences that will translate well into Spanish, French, and German. Avoid idioms, wordplay, and culturally specific references."* The result is easier to translate and often clearer in English, too.

Creative Writing

ChatGPT is a surprisingly capable creative collaborator. It handles:

- **Fiction:** Short stories, flash fiction, novel chapter drafts, dialogue
- **Poetry:** Various forms and styles, from haiku to sonnets to free verse
- **Scripts:** Screenplays, podcast scripts, YouTube video scripts
- **Songs:** Lyrics in various genres and styles

The key to good creative prompts is specificity about style:

"Write a short story (800 words) in the style of Raymond Carver. A couple sits in a diner, not saying what they mean. End on an ambiguous note."

That produces dramatically better output than:

"Write a short story about a couple."

For creative writing, ChatGPT works best as a collaborator, not a ghostwriter. Use it to: - Break through writer's block ("Give me five opening lines for a story about...") - Generate variations ("Rewrite this scene from the antagonist's perspective") - Get unstuck on plot ("My character is trapped in X situation. Give me three possible ways out") - Practice and learn ("Write this in the style of Hemingway. Now explain what makes his style distinctive")

When AI-Written Text Works (and When It Doesn't)

ChatGPT-generated text is appropriate when: - Speed matters more than uniqueness (internal emails, first drafts, routine communication) - The content is factual and functional (product descriptions, FAQs, documentation) - You're using it as a starting point that you'll heavily edit - The audience doesn't care who wrote it (internal memos, notes, lists)

ChatGPT-generated text is problematic when: - Authenticity is the point (personal essays, heartfelt letters, opinion pieces) - You're representing it as entirely your own work in contexts that require disclosure - Accuracy is critical (journalism, academic writing, legal documents) - Your unique voice is what the reader is there for (your blog, your social media, your column)

The line isn't always clear, and reasonable people disagree about where it falls. We explore the ethics of AI-assisted writing more deeply in Chapter 32. For now, a rule of thumb: the more the writing is supposed to represent *you specifically*, the more you should be the one doing the writing, with ChatGPT as assistant rather than author.

Walkthrough: Writing a Professional Bio

Let's put these techniques together with a practical example.

Step 1 — Brief: *"Help me write a professional bio for my company's website. I'm Sarah Chen, VP of Marketing at a B2B SaaS company called Beacon Analytics. We sell data analytics tools to mid-market companies. I've been in marketing for 12 years, previously at HubSpot and Salesforce. I have an MBA from Kellogg. The bio should be third person, professional but approachable, and about 150 words."*

Step 2 — Review the draft and give feedback: *"Good start, but it sounds too corporate. Make it warmer — like something a real person wrote, not a PR team. Also, mention that I'm passionate about making data accessible to non-technical teams."*

Step 3 — Fine-tune: *"Better. Change 'passionate about' to something less cliché. And end with something about what I do outside of work — I run half-marathons and I'm learning to surf."*

Step 4 — Polish it yourself. Read the final version, make your own tweaks, make sure it sounds like you.

This four-step process took about three minutes and produced a bio that would have taken thirty minutes to write from scratch. That's the real value of ChatGPT for writing — not replacement, but acceleration.

In the next chapter, we look at how ChatGPT can transform the way you do research and learn new things.

Chapter 7: Research and Learning

ChatGPT is one of the most powerful learning tools ever created. It explains any topic at any level, answers follow-up questions instantly, summarizes dense material, and guides you through subjects you've never studied before. And with Deep Research, it can run multi-step investigations that used to take hours of manual work.

This chapter shows you how to use ChatGPT for research and learning — and how to avoid the traps that come with relying on an AI that sometimes makes things up.

ChatGPT as a Research Assistant

Traditional research means searching the web, clicking through results, reading multiple sources, evaluating their credibility, and synthesizing what you've found. ChatGPT compresses that process, but it doesn't eliminate the need for critical thinking.

When to use ChatGPT for research: - Getting an overview of a topic you know nothing about - Understanding different perspectives on an issue - Summarizing long documents, papers, or reports - Finding the right questions to ask (before you go deeper) - Synthesizing information from multiple angles

When to be cautious: - Specific facts, statistics, dates, and figures (always verify) - Academic citations (ChatGPT can invent references that don't exist) - Rapidly changing information (use web search mode) - Topics where misinformation is common (health, politics, finance)

The golden rule: **ChatGPT is a starting point, not an endpoint.** Use it to build your understanding, then verify the specifics through authoritative sources.

A practical research workflow: Start by asking ChatGPT for a landscape overview of your topic — the key concepts, the main debates, the important names. Then ask which areas are most relevant to your specific question. Go deep on those areas, asking for details and examples. Finally, use web search to verify the claims that matter most. Wide, then narrow, then verify — that approach consistently produces better results than either ChatGPT-only or search-engine-only research.

Web Search: Getting Current Information

By default, ChatGPT generates responses from its training data, which has a knowledge cutoff. For current information, you need it to search the web.

On paid plans, ChatGPT often detects when a query requires current information and searches automatically. You can also ask explicitly:

"Search the web and tell me what happened at today's Federal Reserve meeting."

"Find the current price of the iPhone 16 Pro at Best Buy."

"What are the latest reviews of the Toyota Camry 2026?"

When ChatGPT searches the web, it provides citations — clickable links to the sources it used. This is important for two reasons: 1. You can verify the information 2. You can go deeper by reading the original sources

Tip: If you want sourced, verifiable answers, ask ChatGPT to search the web rather than relying on its training data. Adding *"search the web for this"* or *"find recent sources"* changes the response from "here's what I learned in training" to "here's what I found right now, with links."

Deep Research

Deep Research is one of ChatGPT's most powerful features, available to Plus and Pro subscribers. It's built for research tasks too complex for a single web search.

When you activate Deep Research, ChatGPT: 1. Reads and analyzes your question 2. Develops a research plan 3. Browses dozens of sources across the web 4. Reads and synthesizes the content it finds 5. Produces a structured report with citations

The process takes several minutes — sometimes longer for complex topics. But the output is remarkably thorough, comparable to what a junior research analyst might produce after several hours of work.

Good Deep Research prompts:

"Research the current state of solid-state battery technology. Who are the leading companies, what are the key technical challenges, and what's the realistic timeline for commercial adoption? Provide citations for all claims."

"Analyze the competitive landscape of project management software for small businesses in 2026. Compare the top five options on features, pricing, and user satisfaction."

"What does the research say about the long-term effects of intermittent fasting? Include both supportive and critical studies."

Tips for Deep Research: - Be specific about what you want to know — vague questions produce vague reports - Specify the depth and format you want ("detailed," "with citations," "compare X and Y") - Let it run — don't interrupt the process - Treat the output as a starting point for your own analysis, not a finished product - Verify the most important citations by clicking through to the sources - Tell it who the audience is — a Deep Research report for your boss looks different than one for your own learning

The honest take on Deep Research: It's one of the features that most clearly justifies the Plus subscription. The reports aren't perfect — they sometimes miss important sources, occasionally mischaracterize a claim, and can lean toward mainstream perspectives at the expense of emerging or contrarian viewpoints. But they're remarkably good starting points. A Deep Research report gives you a structured framework with citations that would take hours to assemble manually. Think of it as a first draft of research from a diligent but fallible assistant — you still need to review and supplement, but the heavy lifting is done.

Comparing Deep Research to regular search: Say you want to understand the current state of electric vehicle battery recycling. A regular ChatGPT query gives you a conversational overview based on training data. A web search query gives you a conversational overview with some current citations. Deep Research browses dozens of pages, cross-references claims, identifies the leading companies and research groups, pulls in recent data points, and delivers a structured report with organized sections and numbered citations. The depth gap is substantial.

Summarizing Documents

One of ChatGPT's most practical research capabilities is document summarization. Upload a file — PDF, Word document, presentation, or even a screenshot of a page — and ask ChatGPT to summarize it.

"Summarize this 30-page report in 5 bullet points."

"What are the three most important findings in this paper?"

"Read this contract and highlight any unusual or concerning clauses."

"Summarize this earnings call transcript. What guidance did management give for next quarter?"

For very long documents, GPT-5.4 performs significantly better than GPT-5.3 — document understanding is one of the areas with the biggest quality gap between models.

Explaining Complex Topics

This is where ChatGPT shines. Its ability to calibrate explanations to your level is remarkable.

The power of "Explain Like I'm..."

"Explain quantum computing like I'm a high school student." "Explain quantum computing like I'm a software engineer who knows classical computing but nothing about quantum." "Explain quantum computing like I'm a physics PhD who wants to understand the engineering challenges."

Each produces a fundamentally different explanation, calibrated to a different starting point. That makes ChatGPT an extraordinary learning tool — it meets you where you are.

Try this yourself: Pick something you've always been curious about but never taken the time to learn — how the Federal Reserve sets interest rates, how mRNA vaccines work, how a car engine converts fuel to motion. Ask ChatGPT to explain it at your level. Then ask follow-ups. In fifteen minutes, you'll have a solid understanding of something that would have taken an hour of Wikipedia articles and YouTube videos. This is ChatGPT at its best.

Building understanding progressively:

You don't have to learn everything in one prompt. Have a conversation:

1. *"Give me a basic overview of how the stock market works."*
2. *"Okay, now explain what an index fund is."*
3. *"How is that different from an ETF?"*
4. *"What's the tax advantage of holding index funds long-term?"*
5. *"Can you walk me through how I'd actually buy one through a brokerage account?"*

Each question builds on the last. ChatGPT remembers the context of the conversation, so it doesn't repeat basics you've already covered. This progressive learning is one of the most valuable ways to use ChatGPT — and it's something a search engine simply can't do.

Study Aids

ChatGPT can generate a wide variety of study materials:

Quizzes: *"Create a 10-question multiple-choice quiz on the causes of World War I. Include the correct answers at the end."*

Flashcards: *"Generate 20 flashcards (question on one side, answer on the other) for introductory microeconomics concepts."*

Practice problems: *"Give me five practice problems on polynomial long division, starting easy and getting progressively harder. Don't show the solutions until I ask."*

Concept maps: *"List the key concepts in cellular biology and explain how they connect to each other."*

Mnemonics and memory aids: *"Create a mnemonic to help me remember the order of the planets."*

Study Mode

Study Mode is a dedicated learning experience within ChatGPT. When activated, it turns ChatGPT from an answer-giving machine into an interactive tutor.

In Study Mode, ChatGPT: - Asks questions to gauge your current understanding - Uses Socratic questioning instead of just giving answers - Scaffolds explanations — building from what you know to what you don't - Runs periodic knowledge checks to reinforce learning - Remembers your progress across sessions - Gives targeted feedback on your weak spots

You can toggle Study Mode on or off during any conversation. It's particularly effective for subjects with clear right and wrong answers — math, science, languages, and test prep.

Interactive Learning

For math and science topics, ChatGPT can now present interactive visual modules that let you experiment with formulas and variables in real time. This launched with over 70 topics, including:

- The Pythagorean theorem
- The ideal gas law
- Circle area and circumference
- Lens equations
- Compound interest formulas

These modules let you adjust inputs, manipulate equations, and instantly see how changes affect graphs and outcomes. It's a fundamentally different way of learning compared to reading a textbook — you build intuition by playing with the concepts.

Fact-Checking: The Critical Skill

We've mentioned this before, but it's important enough to dedicate a section to. ChatGPT will sometimes:

- **Invent facts.** It can generate statistics that don't exist, attribute quotes to people who never said them, and describe events that never happened — all with perfect confidence.
- **Invent citations.** Ask for academic references and it may produce titles, authors, and journal names that look real but are fabricated.

- **Mix accurate and inaccurate information.** A response might be 90% correct with one wrong detail buried in the middle.
- **Present outdated information as current.** Without web search, it may not know about recent developments.

How to protect yourself: 1. **Use web search** for anything that needs to be factually accurate 2. **Ask for sources** and then check them — click the links, verify they exist, verify they say what ChatGPT claims 3. **Cross-reference** important information with authoritative sources 4. **Be especially skeptical** of specific numbers, dates, names, and direct quotes 5. **Ask ChatGPT itself** to flag areas of uncertainty: *"How confident are you in these facts? Which ones should I verify?"*

The goal isn't to distrust ChatGPT entirely — that would make it useless. Trust it proportionally to the stakes. Use its output freely for brainstorming and understanding concepts. Verify rigorously when accuracy matters.

Walkthrough: Researching a Topic for a Presentation

Let's say you need to give a presentation on renewable energy trends to your company's leadership team next week.

Step 1 — Get an overview: *"Give me a high-level overview of the current state of renewable energy in the US. What are the major trends, technologies, and challenges as of 2026?"*

Step 2 — Identify the most interesting angles: *"Which of these trends would be most relevant to a mid-size manufacturing company? We're exploring whether to invest in on-site renewable energy."*

Step 3 — Go deep on the selected topic: *"Tell me more about commercial solar installation for manufacturing facilities. What's the typical ROI timeline, what are the main incentives, and what are the risks?"*

Step 4 — Use Deep Research for current data: *"Use Deep Research to find current data on commercial solar panel costs, federal and state incentives in [your state], and case studies of manufacturing companies that have made this switch. Include citations."*

Step 5 — Create presentation structure: *"Based on everything we've discussed, create a 10-slide outline for a presentation to our leadership team. The goal is to get approval for a feasibility study."*

Step 6 — Draft key slides: *"Write the speaker notes for slides 3 through 5, which cover the financial case."*

In about 30 minutes of conversation, you've gone from knowing nothing about commercial solar to having a structured, data-backed presentation outline. The Deep Research step gives you real data and citations that your leadership team can verify. That's the acceleration ChatGPT makes possible.

Next up: Chapter 8 covers how ChatGPT can help with the everyday tasks that fill your personal life.

Chapter 8: Everyday Productivity

ChatGPT isn't just a work tool. It's useful for the personal tasks that fill your days — planning events, organizing your life, making decisions, getting things done. This chapter covers the everyday use cases where ChatGPT saves you time and mental energy.

Trip Planning

This is one of the most popular personal uses of ChatGPT, and one where it excels. Instead of spending hours on travel blogs and review sites, you can have a conversation:

"Plan a 7-day trip to Portugal for two people in October. We like food, history, and hiking but not nightclubs. Budget is moderate — not backpacker but not luxury. We'll fly into Lisbon."

ChatGPT produces a day-by-day itinerary covering cities, activities, restaurants, transportation, and rough budget estimates. The power is in the follow-ups:

"We actually only have 5 days. What would you cut?" "Add a day trip to Sintra." "What's the best way to get from Lisbon to Porto? Train vs. car?" "Give me restaurant recommendations for each dinner — mid-range, authentic Portuguese food." "What should we pack for October weather?"

Each follow-up refines the plan without starting over. By the end, you have a detailed, personalized travel plan that would have taken hours to assemble from scattered web sources.

Important caveat: Verify specific recommendations. ChatGPT may suggest a restaurant that has closed or a hotel that doesn't exist at the given address. Use its itinerary as a framework, then confirm the specifics on Google Maps, booking sites, and review platforms.

A trip planning tip that saves time: After ChatGPT gives you a multi-day itinerary, ask: *"Now give me a day-by-day packing list based on this itinerary and the expected weather."* Then: *"Create a checklist of things I need to do before the trip — bookings to make, reservations to confirm, documents to* *prepare."* ChatGPT can generate the operational scaffolding around the trip, not just the fun parts. Most people use it for the itinerary and forget it can also handle the logistics.

Another underused trick: Ask ChatGPT to estimate your total trip budget with a breakdown: *"Based on this itinerary, estimate our daily spending for two people: accommodation, food (breakfast, lunch, dinner), transportation between cities, activity admission fees, and miscellaneous. Give ranges for budget, mid-range, and comfortable spending."* This gives you a budget framework before you book anything.

Meal Planning and Recipes

ChatGPT is an endlessly patient sous chef.

Weekly meal planning: *"Create a weekly dinner plan for a family of four. Two adults, two kids (ages 6 and 9). We want: healthy but not weird, at least two vegetarian meals, nothing that takes more than 45 minutes on weeknights, and a more ambitious weekend meal."*

Recipe adaptation: *"Here's my grandmother's lasagna recipe [paste recipe]. Adapt it to be gluten-free without changing the flavor."*

Using what you have: *"I have chicken thighs, sweet potatoes, a can of coconut milk, and some wilting cilantro. What can I make?"*

Dietary needs: *"Give me a high-protein meal prep plan for the week. I'm targeting 150g of protein per day. I don't eat red meat."*

Shopping lists: *"Based on the meal plan you created, generate a shopping list organized by grocery store section."*

ChatGPT doesn't just give you recipes — it understands constraints, substitutions, and preferences. It can scale recipes up or down, convert between measurement systems, and explain techniques you're not familiar with.

What makes ChatGPT better than a recipe site: Recipe sites give you a recipe. ChatGPT gives you a conversation. Say *"What if I don't have coconut milk?"* and get an instant substitution. Say *"I only have 30 minutes, not 45"* and get the recipe adapted for speed. Say *"My kid won't eat mushrooms"* and get them swapped out. This real-time adaptation is what makes ChatGPT more useful for cooking than searching Google for recipes.

Meal prep for the week: If you meal prep on Sundays, try this: *"I want to meal prep five lunches and five dinners for the week. I have a slow cooker and an Instant Pot. Budget: $75 for groceries. I like Mediterranean and Asian flavors. Give me the recipes and a single consolidated shopping list."* The consolidated shopping list — where ingredients used across multiple recipes are combined — saves you from buying three separate bunches of cilantro.

Event and Party Planning

"I'm hosting a dinner party for 8 people. Two are vegetarian, one is gluten-free. Plan a three-course menu that works for everyone without making separate dishes."

"My daughter is turning 7. Plan a birthday party for 15 kids in our backyard. Budget is $300. Include activities, food, and a timeline."

"I'm organizing a team offsite for 12 people. We need a morning activity, lunch, and an afternoon workshop. We're in Austin, Texas. The group is mixed introverts and extroverts."

For any planning task, the pattern is the same: give ChatGPT the constraints (who, how many, where, when, budget, preferences), get a plan, then refine through follow-ups.

Personal Finance Questions

ChatGPT can help you understand financial concepts and think through decisions, though it should never replace a financial advisor for major decisions.

Understanding concepts: *"Explain how a 401(k) match works. My employer matches 50% up to 6% of my salary."*

Comparing options: *"I'm choosing between paying off my student loans (5.5% interest) and investing the money. Walk me through the trade-offs."*

Budgeting: *"Here's my monthly income and expenses [paste details]. Where am I overspending? What's a reasonable savings target?"*

Tax questions: *"What's the difference between a standard deduction and itemizing? How do I know which is better for me?"*

Important: ChatGPT can explain financial concepts and help you think through decisions, but it doesn't know your complete financial picture, and it isn't liable for bad advice. For major financial decisions — investment strategy, tax optimization, estate planning — use ChatGPT to prepare for a conversation with a qualified financial advisor, not to replace one.

Where ChatGPT shines for personal finance: It's at its best when you need to understand something, not when you need to decide something. *"Explain Roth IRA income limits and the backdoor Roth strategy in plain English"* is a perfect ChatGPT question — the explanation will be clearer than most financial websites because you can ask follow-ups until it clicks. *"Should I put my money in a Roth IRA or pay off my student loans?"* is one where ChatGPT can help you think through the factors, but the answer depends on specifics that require a professional to evaluate.

Health and Wellness

ChatGPT can be a useful health information resource with important limitations.

What it's good for: - Explaining medical terms and conditions in plain language - Helping you prepare questions for a doctor's appointment - Understanding medication side effects and interactions (as a starting point) - Creating exercise routines and stretching programs - Understanding nutrition labels and dietary guidelines

What it should *not* be used for: - Self-diagnosis - Deciding whether to take or stop taking medication - Replacing professional medical advice for any condition - Emergency medical situations (call 911 or your local emergency number)

A good use of ChatGPT for health: *"I was just diagnosed with type 2 diabetes. Help me understand what this means, what questions I should ask my doctor at our next appointment, and what dietary changes are typically recommended."*

A dangerous use: *"I have chest pain and shortness of breath. What should I do?"* (The answer is always: seek immediate medical attention.)

Home and DIY

"How do I fix a running toilet? Walk me through the diagnosis step by step."

"I want to paint my living room. The walls are currently dark blue and I want to go to light gray. What's the process? Do I need primer?"

"Create a basic maintenance checklist for a homeowner — what should I check or do monthly, quarterly, and annually?"

"I'm trying to organize my garage. It's a two-car garage with one car, bikes, tools, and a lot of junk. Give me a weekend plan to get it organized."

ChatGPT is excellent at breaking DIY projects into clear steps, listing tools and materials, and helping you anticipate problems. For complex projects (electrical work, plumbing beyond basic fixes, structural changes), it'll often tell you to call a professional — valuable advice in itself.

Decision-Making

One of ChatGPT's most underappreciated uses is helping you think through decisions. It's not making the decision for you — it's helping you structure your thinking.

Pros and cons: *"I'm considering leaving my full-time job to freelance. Help me think through the pros, cons, and risks. For context, I'm a graphic designer, 5 years experience, single, renting, $15K in savings."*

Comparison shopping: *"Compare the top three robot vacuums under $500. I have a dog, hardwood floors, and carpet. What matters most for my situation?"*

Weighing options: *"I got into two MBA programs: one is higher-ranked but in a city I don't love, the other is lower-ranked but has a strong network in the industry I want to work in. Help me think through this."*

ChatGPT won't tell you what to do, but it will surface angles you missed and organize your thinking in a way that makes the decision clearer.

The decision framework prompt: For big decisions, try this pattern: *"I'm deciding between [option A] and [option B]. Here's my situation: [context]. Create a decision matrix that weighs the factors I should consider. Score each* *option on each factor. Then tell me what you'd lean toward and why — but also tell me what would make the other option the right choice."* This gives you structured thinking, a recommendation, and the conditions under which you should override it. It's like having a thoughtful friend walk you through the decision.

Comparison shopping, leveled up: For any purchase over a few hundred dollars, ask ChatGPT to help you think through what matters for your situation before you start comparing products. *"I'm buying a dishwasher. My kitchen is small, I live alone, I cook often but hate noise. What features should I prioritize, and which can I ignore?"* This prevents the common trap of comparing twenty products on features that don't matter to you.

Walkthrough: Planning a Two-Week Trip

Here's a complete example of how a trip planning conversation might unfold:

You: *"My partner and I are planning a two-week trip to Japan in April. First time visiting. We love food, temples, nature, and small towns. We don't love crowds. Budget is about $5,000 total not including flights. We'll fly into Tokyo."*

ChatGPT: [Produces a 14-day itinerary covering Tokyo, Hakone, Kyoto, Nara, Osaka, Hiroshima, and Miyajima, with daily activities, food recommendations, and transportation]

You: *"This looks great but there's too much city time. Can we add more nature? We'd love to hike."*

ChatGPT: [Revises to include Kamakura hiking trails, the Kumano Kodo pilgrimage route, and a night in a mountain ryokan]

You: *"Perfect. Now give me a rough budget breakdown."*

ChatGPT: [Breaks down accommodation, food, transportation, activities, and miscellaneous, with cost-saving tips]

You: *"What about a Japan Rail Pass? Is it worth it for our itinerary?"*

ChatGPT: [Analyzes the specific routes in the itinerary and calculates whether a 14-day JR Pass saves money vs. individual tickets]

You: *"Last thing — what phrases should we learn in Japanese? We want to be polite but we're definitely not going to become fluent."*

ChatGPT: [Provides 20 essential Japanese phrases with pronunciation guides, organized by situation: greetings, restaurants, directions, hotels, and emergencies]

Total time: about 20 minutes. Result: a comprehensive, customized travel plan with budget, logistics, and a phrasebook. Not bad for a conversation.

In the next chapter, we'll look at how ChatGPT can help with your professional life — from meeting prep to job searching to day-to-day work tasks.

Chapter 9: Work and Professional Use

ChatGPT is increasingly a workplace tool. Industry surveys consistently show that over half of knowledge workers now use AI assistants at least weekly, and ChatGPT leads that category by a wide margin. This chapter covers the professional use cases that make the biggest difference in your workday.

Meeting Prep

Meetings are more productive when you walk in prepared. ChatGPT can help you prepare for almost any type of meeting in minutes:

Before a meeting with a new client: *"I'm meeting with the CEO of a mid-size logistics company tomorrow. They're considering our project management software. What questions should I be prepared to answer? What questions should I ask them?"*

Before a strategy meeting: *"We're having a quarterly planning meeting for our marketing team. Our goals are to increase lead generation by 20% and improve conversion rates. Help me create an agenda that keeps the meeting focused and productive. We have 90 minutes."*

Before a difficult conversation: *"I need to have a performance conversation with a team member who's been consistently missing deadlines. Help me plan what to say. I want to be direct but supportive. The goal is improvement, not punishment."*

After a meeting: *"Here are my messy notes from today's meeting [paste notes]. Clean these up into a structured summary with action items, owners, and deadlines."*

The meeting prep most people skip: Beyond content, ChatGPT can help you prepare mentally. *"I'm about to join a budget review meeting where my department's spending is 15% over target. My VP will be there. What tough questions should I expect, and how should I frame my responses?"* Anticipatory preparation — thinking through the hard questions before they're asked — is something ChatGPT excels at because it can consider the situation from multiple angles without the emotional baggage you bring to it.

Turning meeting notes into follow-ups: After the meeting, paste your notes and ask: *"Based on these notes, draft a follow-up email to the attendees. Summarize the decisions made, list action items with owners, and note the next meeting date. Tone: professional, brief, clear."* This turns a 15-minute post-meeting task into a 2-minute review-and-send.

Reports and Proposals

ChatGPT is excellent at creating the structure and first draft of business documents:

Report structure: *"Create an outline for a quarterly business review. We're a SaaS company. Include sections for revenue, growth metrics, customer satisfaction, product updates, and next quarter's priorities."*

Executive summaries: *"Here's our 20-page market research report [upload file]. Write a one-page executive summary for our board of directors. Focus on the findings that require strategic decisions."*

Proposals: *"Draft a project proposal for implementing a CRM system at our company. We have 50 employees, a sales team of 12, and we're currently using spreadsheets. Budget is $50K for the first year. The audience is our CFO."*

Business cases: *"Help me build a business case for hiring two additional customer support agents. Our current metrics: average response time is 4 hours, customer satisfaction is 3.6/5, and we're losing roughly 5 customers per month who cite poor support. Cost of two new hires is approximately $120K/year fully loaded."*

For any business document, tell ChatGPT who the audience is and what decision you want them to make. This shapes the entire document — the language, the emphasis, and the data that gets highlighted.

The audience trick that transforms business writing: The same information lands differently depending on who's reading it. Try this. Give ChatGPT the same project update and ask for three versions: one for your direct manager (detailed, tactical), one for the VP (strategic, focused on impact), and one for the board (high-level, focused on business outcomes). You'll see the same facts reframed for each audience. This is a skill that takes years to develop — ChatGPT gives you a shortcut to audience-appropriate communication.

A prompt for proposals that get approved: *"Draft a one-page proposal for [project]. The decision-maker is our CFO, who cares about ROI and risk management. Structure it as: Problem (one paragraph), Proposed Solution (one paragraph), Expected Impact with specific numbers, Required Investment, Risk Mitigation, and Timeline. The goal is to get approval to proceed with a pilot."*

This format — problem, solution, numbers, risk, timeline — works for almost any business proposal because it answers the questions decision-makers actually ask.

Data Analysis and Spreadsheets

You don't need to be a data analyst to use ChatGPT for data work. Upload a CSV, Excel file, or even paste data directly, and ChatGPT can:

Analyze: *"Here's our sales data for the last 12 months [upload file]. What are the main trends? Which products are growing and which are declining?"*

Visualize: *"Create a chart showing monthly revenue by product line."*

Transform: *"Clean up this data. Remove duplicates, standardize the date format, and flag any rows with missing values."*

Calculate: *"What's our customer churn rate for each quarter? Show me the calculation."*

Formulas: *"Write an Excel formula that looks up a product name in column A and returns the sum of all sales for that product from the sales table on Sheet 2."*

With GPT-5.4, ChatGPT can even create and edit spreadsheets directly — building them from scratch based on your requirements. We'll cover this in more detail in Chapter 15.

Brainstorming and Ideation

When you need ideas — for products, campaigns, solutions, or strategies — ChatGPT is an inexhaustible brainstorming partner.

Volume: *"Give me 30 content ideas for our company blog. We sell cybersecurity software to small businesses."*

Constraints: *"We need a team-building activity for 20 people that's remote-friendly, takes less than an hour, costs nothing, and isn't another Zoom quiz."*

Reframing: *"Our customer acquisition cost is too high. Give me ten unconventional ways to acquire customers that don't involve paid advertising."*

Devil's advocate: *"Here's our plan for the product launch [describe plan]. Play devil's advocate. What could go wrong? What are we not thinking about?"*

The devil's advocate prompt is especially valuable. ChatGPT doesn't have the political dynamics of your team — it won't hesitate to flag risks a colleague might stay quiet about.

The "pre-mortem" technique: Before launching a project, ask ChatGPT: *"Imagine this project failed six months from now. Write the post-mortem. What went wrong?"* Top strategists use this technique, and ChatGPT is an ideal partner because it can imagine failure scenarios without the optimism bias that affects the team building the project. The resulting list of risks is often uncomfortably accurate — and therefore extremely valuable.

Job Search

ChatGPT can assist with every phase of the job search process:

Resumes

"Here's my resume [paste or upload]. I'm applying for a senior product manager role at [company]. Review my resume through the eyes of a hiring manager at that company. What's strong? What's missing?"

"Rewrite my experience bullets to focus more on impact and results rather than responsibilities."

"I'm transitioning from finance to product management. Help me reframe my experience to highlight transferable skills."

Cover Letters

"Write a cover letter for [specific role at specific company]. I'm [brief background]. My key selling points are [list them]. The tone should be confident but not arrogant. Keep it to one page."

Always customize the output. A generic AI cover letter is worse than no cover letter. But ChatGPT gives you a strong structure and phrasing that you can personalize.

Interview Prep

"What are the most common interview questions for a [role] position? Give me 15 questions and brief guidance on how to answer each one."

"I have a behavioral interview tomorrow. Give me the STAR format and help me practice. Here's the job description [paste it]. Ask me questions one at a time and give me feedback on my answers."

This is one of the most valuable uses of ChatGPT for job seekers. It's a patient interview coach that simulates different interview styles and gives constructive feedback.

"I'm going to practice answering interview questions. You be the interviewer. The role is [describe role]. Start with a general question, then get progressively more technical. After each answer, give me honest feedback."

The salary research prompt most people miss: *"Search the web for current salary data for [role] in [city/region]. Include data from at least three sources (Glassdoor, Levels.fyi, Payscale, or similar). Consider [X years of experience] and [relevant skills/certifications]. What's the 25th, 50th, and 75th percentile?"*

Walking into a negotiation with sourced salary data from multiple platforms changes the dynamic entirely. ChatGPT compiles this in minutes.

Salary Negotiation

"I've been offered $115K for a senior software engineer role in Austin. Based on current market data, is that competitive? How should I approach the negotiation? The company seems really interested in me."

"Draft a response to this offer that expresses enthusiasm but opens the door to negotiation on salary and equity."

Communication at Work

Difficult emails: *"Write an email declining a project that I don't have bandwidth for. The requester is a VP in another department. I need to say no without damaging the relationship."*

Upward communication: *"Help me draft a status update for my director. Key points: Project A is on track, Project B is delayed by two weeks due to a vendor issue, I need a decision on budget for Project C by Friday."*

Cross-cultural communication: *"I'm emailing business partners in Japan for the first time. What cultural norms should I be aware of in business email communication?"*

Delivering bad news: *"Draft a message to our customers about a price increase. We're raising prices by 15% effective next month. We need to be transparent about the reason (costs) while emphasizing the value we provide."*

Walkthrough: Preparing for a Job Interview

Let's walk through a complete interview prep session.

Step 1 — Research the company: *"Tell me about [company]. What do they do, what's their culture like, and what have they been in the news for recently? Search the web for current information."*

Step 2 — Analyze the job description: *"Here's the job description [paste it]. What are the three most important things this employer is looking for? What skills or experiences should I emphasize?"*

Step 3 — Prepare your stories: *"Based on the job description, what behavioral interview questions are most likely? Give me five. For each one, help me structure a strong answer using my background: [brief summary of your experience]."*

Step 4 — Practice: *"Let's do a mock interview. Ask me these questions one at a time. After each answer, give me feedback on what was strong and what I should improve."*

Step 5 — Prepare your questions: *"Give me five thoughtful questions to ask at the end of the interview that demonstrate genuine interest in the role and the company."*

Step 6 — Handle curveballs: *"What's the hardest question I might get asked in this interview? How should I handle it?"*

This prep takes about 30 minutes with ChatGPT and covers research, preparation, practice, and strategy. Most candidates walk into interviews with far less.

A Note on AI at Work

If your company has an AI usage policy, read it before using ChatGPT for work tasks. Many organizations have guidelines about:

- What types of information can be shared with AI tools
- Whether ChatGPT output needs to be disclosed
- Which plans are approved (many companies require Business or Enterprise for data privacy)
- Specific use cases that are allowed or prohibited

If your company doesn't have a policy yet, err on the side of caution: don't share confidential information, trade secrets, proprietary code, or personal data about customers or colleagues with ChatGPT unless you're on a Business or Enterprise plan with appropriate data protections.

We'll dive deeper into workplace AI policy and ethics in Chapters 28 and 32.

Part II is complete. Starting with Chapter 10, we'll explore the creative tools that make ChatGPT more than just a text tool — starting with image generation.

Part III: Creative Tools

"Creativity is intelligence having fun."

— Albert Einstein

Chapter 10: Image Generation with DALL-E

ChatGPT can create images from text descriptions using DALL-E, OpenAI's image generation model. Describe what you want — a logo concept, a social media graphic, an illustration for a presentation, a piece of art — and ChatGPT will create it for you.

Image generation is available on Plus, Pro, Business, and Enterprise plans. Free and Go users have limited or no access.

How It Works

You don't need to invoke a special tool or mode. Just ask ChatGPT to create an image:

"Create an image of a cozy coffee shop on a rainy day, seen through a window."

"Generate a minimalist logo for a company called 'Greenline' that makes sustainable packaging."

"Draw a diagram showing how photosynthesis works, in a style suitable for a children's textbook."

ChatGPT routes your request to DALL-E automatically, generates the image, and displays it in the conversation. You can then ask for modifications, variations, or entirely new images.

Writing Effective Image Prompts

The quality of your image depends heavily on how you describe it. Here's what to include:

Subject: What's in the image. **Style:** Photography, illustration, watercolor, digital art, 3D render, pixel art, etc. **Mood:** Warm, dramatic, playful, minimalist, dark, vibrant. **Composition:** Close-up, wide shot, bird's-eye view, centered, off-center. **Color palette:** Specific colors, warm tones, muted pastels, high contrast. **Details:** Lighting, textures, background, time of day.

Compare these prompts:

Basic: *"A mountain."*

Detailed: *"A snow-capped mountain at golden hour, reflected in a perfectly still alpine lake. Photo-realistic style, warm tones, dramatic sky with wispy clouds. Wide landscape composition."*

The second prompt gives DALL-E enough information to produce something specific and compelling. The first will produce something generic.

A prompt formula that works consistently: Start with the subject, add the style, then layer in the details: *"[Subject] in [style], with [mood/atmosphere], [composition], [color palette], [any specific details]."* For example: *"A cozy bookshop interior in watercolor style, warm golden lighting, bookshelves floor to ceiling, a cat sleeping on a stack of books, autumn leaves visible through the window, muted earth tones with pops of amber."*

What most people get wrong: The biggest mistake beginners make is being too brief. *"A dog"* gives DALL-E almost nothing to work with. *"A golden retriever puppy sitting in a sunlit meadow, photorealistic, shallow depth of field, warm afternoon light, wildflowers in the foreground"* gives it a clear vision to execute. Think of yourself as a film director describing a shot — the more specific your vision, the closer the result.

Another common mistake: Packing too many subjects into one image. *"A city with mountains and a beach and a forest and a castle and a dragon"* produces a cluttered, confused image. DALL-E works best with one clear focal point and supporting details around it.

Iterating on Images

Just like text, you can refine images through conversation:

"Make the sky more dramatic — add storm clouds." "Remove the person on the left." "Make this in a flat illustration style instead of photorealistic." "Keep the same composition but change it to nighttime." "Make the colors warmer."

ChatGPT remembers the context of what you've been creating, so you can build on previous images without re-describing everything from scratch.

How iteration works in practice: Expect 3–5 rounds of refinement to get an image you're happy with. The first generation gets the concept right. The second corrects what's off. The third fine-tunes the details. Professional designers iterate endlessly, and DALL-E is no different. Don't settle for the first output unless it happens to be exactly right.

Edge case: Sometimes DALL-E interprets your refinement request by generating an entirely new image rather than modifying the existing one. If this happens, try being more specific about what to keep: *"Keep the exact same composition and scene. Only change the sky from clear to stormy."* Anchoring the request to what should stay the same helps maintain consistency across iterations.

Style References

DALL-E can produce images in a wide range of artistic styles:

- **Photorealistic** — Indistinguishable from a photograph
- **Digital illustration** — Clean, modern graphic art
- **Watercolor** — Soft, organic, painterly
- **Oil painting** — Rich textures and classical feel
- **Flat design** — Minimalist, geometric, great for icons and infographics
- **Pixel art** — Retro, 8-bit aesthetic
- **3D render** — Smooth, dimensional, product-visualization style
- **Line drawing** — Simple, elegant, pen-and-ink feel
- **Anime/manga** — Japanese animation style
- **Isometric** — 3D perspective on a 2D plane, popular for tech illustrations

Specify the style in your prompt: *"Create a watercolor illustration of..."* or *"Generate a flat-design icon for..."*

Mixing styles for unique results: Combine styles for creative effects: *"A city skyline in the style of a Japanese woodblock print"* or *"A portrait of a cat in the style of a Warhol screen print."* These cross-pollination prompts often produce the most interesting images because they push DALL-E beyond its default interpretation.

Using reference descriptions: If you have a specific aesthetic in mind but can't name it, describe the characteristics: *"The color palette of a Wes Anderson film — pastels, symmetry, and vintage warmth"* or *"The atmosphere of a rainy Edward Hopper painting."* DALL-E understands cultural references and translates them into visual styles.

Practical Use Cases

Presentations: Create custom illustrations, diagrams, and header images instead of using generic stock photos.

Social media: Generate eye-catching visuals for posts, stories, and ads without a design team.

Brainstorming: Quickly visualize product concepts, room layouts, or design ideas.

Personal projects: Custom art for invitations, greeting cards, book covers, or gifts.

Education: Create illustrations for teaching materials, visual aids, and handouts.

Prototyping: Mock up app screens, website layouts, or product designs before hiring a designer.

Practical prompts to try right now:

"Create a flat-design icon set of six icons for a fitness app: home, workout, nutrition, progress, profile, and settings. Use a consistent style with rounded edges and a teal and coral color scheme."

"Generate a book cover concept for a mystery novel titled 'The Last Witness.' Dark, atmospheric, with a single streetlight illuminating an empty bench. Typography should be bold and slightly ominous."

"Create a social media header image for a bakery called 'Morning Rise.' Photorealistic style, showing artisan bread on a wooden board with flour

dusting, warm morning light, shallow depth of field. 1792x1024 landscape format."

Each of these prompts demonstrates a different use case and includes enough detail to produce something usable — or close enough to refine in one or two follow-ups.

What DALL-E Can't Do Well

Text in images. DALL-E has historically struggled with text — words in generated images are often misspelled or garbled. This has improved with recent versions, but always check text carefully.

Exact specifications. DALL-E generates images at fixed resolutions (such as 1024x1024, 1024x1792, and 1792x1024) — it cannot produce images at arbitrary dimensions like 1200x630. It also can't guarantee exact brand colors (e.g., #2D5BFF). For production-ready assets with exact specifications, use DALL-E output as a reference and recreate it in design software.

Consistency across images. If you need the same character or object to look identical across multiple images, DALL-E can get close but won't be pixel-perfect. It generates each image independently.

Photorealistic human faces. While DALL-E can generate realistic-looking people, the results can sometimes fall into the uncanny valley. It also has intentional limitations around generating images of real, identifiable people.

Copyright and Usage Rights

Content you create with DALL-E through ChatGPT is yours to use, including for commercial purposes. OpenAI's terms give you the rights to the images you generate, regardless of your plan tier.

However, there are important nuances:

- You cannot use DALL-E to generate images that infringe on others' copyrights or trademarks
- AI-generated images currently exist in a legal gray area regarding copyright protection — the images may not be copyrightable in all jurisdictions

- Some stock photo platforms and design contests don't accept AI-generated images
- Disclosure norms are evolving — in some contexts, you should indicate that an image was AI-generated

For business use, DALL-E images work well for internal documents, social media, brainstorming, and supplementary visuals. For your primary brand identity (your actual logo, your website's hero images), consider using DALL-E for concepting and then working with a designer for the final versions.

The honest take on DALL-E for business: DALL-E handles the 90% of visual needs that don't require pixel-perfect precision. Need a header image for a blog post? A visual for a presentation? Social media graphics? Concept art for a product pitch? DALL-E handles all of these well enough to use directly, saving you from stock photo subscriptions and graphic designer invoices for routine visual work. But for the 10% that matters most — your logo, your product packaging, your brand campaign imagery — use DALL-E to explore concepts and then hand the best one to a designer to execute at production quality.

Walkthrough: Creating a Logo Concept

Step 1: *"I'm starting a dog walking business called 'Happy Trails Pet Care.' Create five different logo concepts. I want them to feel friendly, professional, and outdoorsy. Use warm earth tones."*

Step 2: *"I like the third one best — the one with the paw print and trail. Can you make three variations of that concept? One more minimalist, one more playful, and one more premium/upscale."*

Step 3: *"The minimalist version is close. Make the paw print slightly larger, change the green to a sage green, and try it with a sans-serif font."*

Step 4: Take the concept you like to a graphic designer and say, "I want something like this." You've just saved hours of back-and-forth trying to describe your vision in words.

Tips and Edge Cases

Aspect ratios matter. DALL-E generates images at specific aspect ratios. For social media headers, request landscape (1792x1024). For Instagram posts, request square (1024x1024). For phone wallpapers or Pinterest pins, request portrait (1024x1792). Specifying the right ratio in your prompt prevents you from getting a beautifully generated image that doesn't fit where you need it.

Negative prompting. You can tell DALL-E what to avoid: *"A modern office space, no people, no computers, just the architecture and furniture."* Or: *"A logo for a tech company. Do not include any cliches like lightbulbs, gears, or circuit boards."* Telling DALL-E what to exclude is sometimes more effective than only describing what to include.

Image editing from uploaded photos. Upload an existing image and ask DALL-E to modify it: *"Take this photo of my living room and show me what it would look like with blue walls instead of white."* Or: *"Here's a photo of our product. Create a version with a clean white background suitable for an e-commerce listing."* Results aren't always perfect, but for quick visualization — seeing how a room might look with different paint, or how a product might look in different settings — it's faster than any alternative.

Using DALL-E for reference images. Even when DALL-E can't produce your final image, it's useful for creating reference images. Need to explain a concept to a designer? Generate a DALL-E image close to what you want and annotate it. Need to visualize how a room might look with different furniture? Generate options. Need to see a product concept before investing in a prototype? DALL-E gives you a visual starting point far more useful than verbal description.

Saving and organizing your images. ChatGPT doesn't save generated images to your device — you need to download them. Get in the habit of downloading images you like immediately. They persist in your conversation history, but finding a specific image from last month's conversations is tedious. Create a folder for DALL-E outputs and save anything worth keeping right away.

Image generation is just one of ChatGPT's creative capabilities. In the next chapter, we'll explore video creation with Sora.

Chapter 11: Video with Sora

Sora is OpenAI's video generation model, integrated into ChatGPT for Plus and Pro subscribers. It turns text descriptions into short video clips — no camera, no editing software, no production skills.

Video generation is the newest of ChatGPT's creative capabilities, and it's evolving rapidly. This chapter covers what Sora can do today and how to use it effectively.

What Sora Can Create

Type a description, and Sora generates a video clip:

"A golden retriever running through a field of wildflowers in slow motion, cinematic lighting."

"A time-lapse of a city skyline transitioning from day to night, rain starting to fall."

"An animated explainer showing how a solar panel converts sunlight to electricity."

Sora produces smooth, high-quality clips — typically 1080p, ranging from a few seconds to about a minute depending on complexity and plan tier. The results can be surprisingly cinematic.

What's impressive: The lighting, atmosphere, and camera movement in Sora's output is often better than a casual video shoot. A prompt like *"Aerial drone shot of a winding river through autumn forest, golden light, slow push forward"* produces footage that looks like it was captured by a professional drone operator — no drone, no location scouting, no golden-hour scheduling. For concept videos, mood reels, and social content, this is a meaningful capability.

What's still rough: People. Complex human movement, detailed facial expressions, and realistic hand gestures remain challenging. If your video needs a person doing something specific (giving a presentation, cooking, shaking hands), the results will likely look uncanny. For now, Sora works best with landscapes, objects, abstract concepts, and atmospheric shots. Scenes with people work better when the camera is distant or the action is simple — a silhouette walking on a beach is more reliable than a close-up of someone talking.

How to Use It

Like image generation, you don't need to activate a special mode. Simply describe the video you want in your ChatGPT conversation:

"Create a video of..." "Generate a short clip showing..." "Make a video that..."

ChatGPT will process your request through Sora and return the video, which you can download, share, or iterate on.

Writing Effective Video Prompts

Video prompts follow similar principles to image prompts but add the dimension of time and motion:

What happens: Describe the action or sequence of events. **Visual style:** Live-action, animation, cinematic, documentary, abstract. **Camera work:** Static shot, pan, zoom, tracking shot, aerial view. **Mood and lighting:** Warm, cool, dramatic, soft, natural. **Duration and pacing:** Fast-paced, slow motion, time-lapse.

Example of a detailed video prompt: *"A steaming cup of coffee on a wooden table by a window. It's early morning — soft golden light streams in. The camera slowly pushes in. Raindrops are visible on the windowpane. Cozy, warm atmosphere. 10 seconds, slow pace."*

Practical Use Cases

Social media content: Create eye-catching video posts, stories, and reels without filming or editing.

Presentations: Add short video clips to presentations to illustrate concepts or transitions.

Product visualization: Show how a product might look in use before it's manufactured.

Concept videos: Create mood boards and visual concepts for film, advertising, or creative projects.

Education: Generate visual demonstrations of scientific concepts, historical events, or processes.

Personal: Create unique video messages, event invitations, or artistic projects.

Practical prompts to try:

"Create a 10-second product showcase: a sleek wireless headphone sitting on a marble surface, slowly rotating, with soft studio lighting and a clean white background. Subtle reflections on the marble. Professional product video feel."

"Generate a 15-second animated explainer showing data flowing from a user's phone through a cloud server and back, using a flat design style with blue and white tones. Simple, clean, suitable for a tech company website."

"Create a nature scene: cherry blossom petals falling in slow motion in a Japanese garden, koi fish visible in a pond below, soft afternoon light filtering through the trees. 10 seconds, meditative pace."

These prompts demonstrate Sora's strongest areas: product visualization, simple animation, and atmospheric nature footage. Notice how each one specifies duration, visual style, lighting, and camera behavior — the same principles that make DALL-E prompts work well apply to Sora, with the addition of time, motion, and camera direction.

Current Limitations

Sora is impressive but still has clear boundaries:

Physics and consistency. Objects may behave unrealistically — limbs can bend wrong, liquids may defy gravity, and shadows might not match the light source.

Human movement. Complex human actions (dancing, sports, detailed hand movements) can look unnatural. Simple actions like walking or sitting are more reliable.

Text and logos. Like DALL-E, Sora struggles with rendering readable text within video.

Length. Videos are currently limited to relatively short clips. It's not going to produce a five-minute short film from a single prompt.

Consistency across clips. If you need multiple clips that look like they belong together (same character, same setting), maintaining visual consistency is challenging.

Processing time. Video generation takes longer than image generation — expect to wait a few minutes for your clip. Complex scenes with multiple elements or specific camera movements take longer than simple ones.

Audio. Sora generates visual footage only — no sound. If you need background music, voiceover, or sound effects, add them in post-production. This is why the "Sora footage plus human post-production" workflow is so common — the visual generation is automated, but the audio layer requires human choices.

Editing and Extending

You can iterate on Sora output through conversation:

"That's close, but make the camera movement slower." "Change the time of day to sunset." "Make it animated instead of photorealistic." "Extend the clip to 15 seconds."

While you can't do frame-by-frame editing within ChatGPT, you can refine the overall concept, style, and mood through follow-up prompts.

A practical editing workflow: Since Sora can't do precise edits, iterate on the full clip. Generate, evaluate, then regenerate with adjusted instructions. Expect 2–4 iterations. Save every version — sometimes your second-favorite has an element you want to reference in later prompts. Keep prompts consistent between iterations, changing only the specific thing you want to adjust. Changing too many variables at once makes it hard to isolate what improved and what regressed.

Combining Sora with other tools: Sora generates raw footage, but you'll often want text overlays, transitions, or music. Download the clip and import it into a video editor — even a free one like CapCut or iMovie. Sora produces the visual foundation; your editing software handles the finishing touches. This workflow (AI-generated footage plus human-edited post-production) is becoming standard for social media creators.

Usage Rights

Like DALL-E images, videos you create with Sora through ChatGPT are yours to use, including commercially. The same caveats apply regarding the evolving legal landscape around AI-generated content.

Walkthrough: Creating a Social Media Video

Step 1: *"Create a 10-second video of a coffee cup on a marble countertop. Steam rises from the cup. Morning light comes through a window on the left. Warm, cozy atmosphere. Camera slowly pushes in."*

Step 2: Review the result. The mood is right but the lighting is too bright.

Step 3: *"Make the lighting softer and warmer — more golden hour, less midday. Keep everything else the same."*

Step 4: *"Now create a version with text overlay that says 'Monday mornings, sorted.' Clean sans-serif font, bottom center."*

Step 5: Download the final clip and post it to your Instagram story.

Total time: about 10 minutes. No camera, no lighting setup, no editing software, no stock footage subscription.

Sora vs. Stock Video

Aspect	Sora	Stock Video
Customization	Exactly what you describe	Limited to what exists
Cost	Included with Plus/Pro	Per-clip or subscription
Speed	Minutes	Browse, download, edit
Quality	Good and improving	Professional-grade
Consistency	Challenging across clips	Varies by library
Uniqueness	One-of-a-kind	Others may use same clip

For quick social content and concepting, Sora wins on speed and customization. For polished, professional-grade video (corporate videos, advertisements, cinematic content), stock footage and professional production remain superior — for now.

The honest assessment of when to use each: Quick video for an Instagram story, concept video for a pitch, visual for a presentation — Sora. TV commercial, corporate brand video, or anything that will be scrutinized closely — professional production. B-roll for a YouTube video — try Sora first, fall back to stock if the quality isn't there. The best creators use both, picking the right tool for each need rather than committing to one.

Sora on Plus vs. Pro

If you're on Plus, you get a limited number of Sora generations per month. Pro users get significantly higher limits. On Plus, be deliberate. Refine your prompts thoroughly (in your head or on paper) before hitting generate. On Pro, you can experiment more freely — generating variations, trying different styles, iterating aggressively.

A cost-conscious workflow for Plus users: Write your video prompt in regular chat first: *"I'm going to create a Sora video. Before I generate it, review this prompt and suggest improvements for the best possible result: [your prompt]."* ChatGPT can refine the prompt before you spend a generation on it — catching vague descriptions, suggesting better camera directions, and recommending style specifications you missed.

The Bigger Picture

Sora represents the beginning of AI video creation, not the mature product. Think of it today as a tool for concepting, social content, and visual exploration rather than a replacement for professional video production. The pace of improvement is rapid — Sora will be significantly more capable six months from now than it is today.

Tips for Better Sora Results

Start simple and add complexity. Your first prompt should describe the core scene clearly. Add style, camera, and mood details in a second version if the basic concept works. Specifying everything at once often produces confused results.

Watch your own results for patterns. After 5–10 videos, you'll notice what Sora handles well and where it struggles. Lean into its strengths (atmospheric scenes, smooth camera movements, natural lighting) and avoid its weaknesses (complex human movement, readable text, precise object interactions).

Be specific about camera movement. The difference between "camera slowly pushes in" and "static shot" changes the feel of the video. Sora responds well to standard cinematography terms: dolly in, pan left, tracking shot, aerial view, close-up, wide shot. If you're not familiar with these, try: *"What are the most common camera movements in cinematography? Give me a brief description of each."* ChatGPT will explain them, and you can use the terminology in your next Sora prompt.

Set realistic expectations. Sora is impressive for a tool that generates video from text in minutes. It's not a replacement for professional video production — yet. Use it for what it's great at today (concepting, social content, B-roll, visual exploration) and watch the space evolve. Six months from now, the quality will be noticeably better.

Next, we'll look at Canvas — ChatGPT's collaborative workspace for writing and editing longer pieces of work.

Chapter 12: Canvas — Collaborative Editing

Canvas is ChatGPT's workspace for longer pieces of writing and code. Instead of working in the chat interface — where everything is a series of messages — Canvas opens a side-by-side editor where you and ChatGPT can collaborate on a document or codebase in real time.

When to Use Canvas vs. Chat

Use the standard chat when: - You have a quick question - You want a short piece of text (an email, a paragraph, a list) - You're brainstorming or having a conversation - The output is something you'll copy and use elsewhere

Use Canvas when: - You're working on a longer document (article, report, essay, proposal) - You want to edit specific sections without regenerating the whole thing - You're writing or editing code - You need to iterate on a document through multiple revisions - You want to see the current state of your work alongside the chat

Opening Canvas

You can open Canvas in several ways: - Ask ChatGPT to use Canvas: *"Open Canvas and let's write a blog post together"* - ChatGPT may suggest Canvas automatically when it detects you're working on a longer piece - Click the Canvas icon if it appears in the interface

Once Canvas opens, you'll see a split view: the chat on one side and the document or code editor on the other.

A tip for getting Canvas to open when you want it: Sometimes ChatGPT responds in the chat when you wanted Canvas. Be explicit: *"Open Canvas and write..."* works more reliably than *"Write a blog post about..."* which might stay in the chat. Once Canvas is open for a conversation, it tends to stay in Canvas mode for subsequent requests. If Canvas opens when you didn't want it — say, for a short email — close it and continue in the chat.

Working with Documents in Canvas

Canvas feels like a collaborative Google Doc with an AI partner. You can:

Edit directly. Click anywhere in the document and type. Your edits are yours — ChatGPT doesn't overwrite them unless you ask.

Highlight and request changes. Select a paragraph and tell ChatGPT what to do with it: *"Make this section more concise"* or *"Add an example here."*

Request global changes. Ask ChatGPT to modify the entire document: *"Change the tone throughout to be more formal"* or *"Add transitions between all sections."*

Add content. Ask ChatGPT to expand specific sections: *"Add a section about pricing between the features section and the FAQ."*

Get feedback. Ask ChatGPT to review what you've written: *"Read through this and tell me what's weak or missing."* The review-before-edit approach is underrated — a diagnostic before making changes prevents you from fixing the wrong things.

Upload files. You can upload reference documents that ChatGPT can use while helping you write. For example, upload a competitor's blog post and ask ChatGPT to write something better. Or upload your company's style guide so Canvas-based writing automatically follows your brand voice.

Undo and redo. Canvas supports undo, so if ChatGPT makes a change you don't like, you can revert it without losing your place. This makes experimentation safe — you can ask ChatGPT to try a bold rewrite and easily undo it if it goes too far.

Working with Code in Canvas

Canvas includes a code editor with syntax highlighting, making it useful for programming tasks:

- Write new code from a description
- Debug existing code by pasting it into Canvas
- Refactor code with ChatGPT's help

- Add comments and documentation
- Convert code between languages

The code editor supports multiple programming languages and provides a more comfortable environment than working with code blocks in the chat.

Why Canvas is better for code: In regular chat, code appears in code blocks embedded in messages. To modify one function in a 200-line file, ChatGPT has to regenerate the entire code block. In Canvas, it can edit just the specific function while leaving everything else untouched. Faster, more precise, easier to follow. For any coding work beyond quick snippets, Canvas should be your default.

A practical code workflow in Canvas: 1. Describe what you want: *"Write a Python script that reads a CSV file, calculates the average of each numeric column, and outputs the results to a new CSV."* 2. Review the code in the editor. Click on a specific function and ask: *"Add error handling for missing files and empty columns."* 3. Highlight the import section and ask: *"Are all these imports necessary?"* 4. Ask: *"Add comments explaining each major section."* 5. Copy the finished code to your project.

Each step modifies the code in place. You never lose track of the current state, and you can edit directly alongside ChatGPT's changes.

Canvas vs. Chat: A Practical Example

Imagine you're writing a company blog post.

In chat: You ask ChatGPT to write the post. It produces the full text in a chat message. You read it, ask for changes, ChatGPT regenerates the entire post. Each revision is a new message, and comparing versions means scrolling up and down. After several rounds, the conversation is long and hard to follow.

In Canvas: You ask ChatGPT to write the post. It appears in the editor panel. You read it, edit parts directly, and ask ChatGPT to rework specific sections. The document evolves in place — no scrolling, no regeneration of parts you already liked. You see the current state at all times.

For anything more than a couple of paragraphs, Canvas is the better experience.

When Canvas really shines: The gap between Canvas and regular chat becomes most apparent on the third or fourth round of revisions. In chat, by the fourth revision, you're scrolling through a long conversation hunting for the latest version among multiple regenerated copies. In Canvas, the document is right there — current, clean, editable. You never wonder "which version is the latest?" because there's only one, and it's the one in the editor.

Canvas for collaboration with others: If you're working on a document with a colleague, Canvas provides a useful intermediate step. Draft and refine in Canvas until it's close to final, then copy it to Google Docs or Word for review. This is faster than drafting in Google Docs from scratch because you get ChatGPT's speed for the first 80% of the work, then switch to your collaboration tools for the final polish.

Tips for Canvas

Be specific about what to change. Instead of "make it better," try "strengthen the opening paragraph, add data to section three, and make the conclusion more actionable."

Edit it yourself too. Canvas is a collaboration tool. Don't just give instructions — jump in and edit directly. The best results come from combining your judgment with ChatGPT's speed.

Use it for revision, not just creation. Paste in your own writing and use Canvas to polish it. This is often more effective than having ChatGPT write from scratch.

Start with structure, fill in later. A powerful Canvas workflow: ask ChatGPT to create a document with section headers, key bullet points, and placeholder text. Then work through each section, replacing the placeholders with real content — some you write yourself, some you ask ChatGPT to expand. The structure-first approach ensures the document is well-organized before any content is written, and it gives you natural stopping points to review progress.

Save your work. Canvas documents exist within the conversation. To preserve your work outside ChatGPT, copy or download it. This matters — if you spend an hour refining a document in Canvas and lose your browser session, the work is saved within the conversation but there's no separate "file." Make it a habit to copy the finished product to your actual document storage (Google Docs, Word, local files) when you're done.

Use version awareness. Canvas doesn't have a formal version history, but you can create informal checkpoints by asking ChatGPT: *"Before we make the next round of changes, save the current version as a reference. If I want to go back, I'll ask for the 'checkpoint version.'"* This gives you a rollback point if the next set of changes takes things in a direction you don't like.

Walkthrough: Writing a Report in Canvas

Step 1: *"Open Canvas. I need to write a quarterly progress report for my team. Sections: Executive Summary, Key Accomplishments, Challenges, and Next Quarter Priorities."*

Step 2: ChatGPT drafts the structure with placeholder content. You start filling in the Key Accomplishments section with your own bullet points, directly in the editor.

Step 3: You highlight the Executive Summary and tell ChatGPT: *"Write this based on the accomplishments and challenges I've filled in below."*

Step 4: You read the summary, edit one sentence yourself, and then ask: *"Make the Challenges section more diplomatic — my VP will read this."*

Step 5: *"Add a data table showing our three KPIs with Q3 actuals vs. targets."*

Step 6: Final review — you read the full document in the editor, make a few last tweaks, and copy it into your company's reporting system.

Total time: 15 minutes. The key difference from chat: you never lost sight of the document. Every change — yours and ChatGPT's — happened in the same living document.

Common Canvas Workflows

The "expand and refine" workflow: Start with a brief outline — section headers and key points. Put it in Canvas. Work through each section one at a time: *"Expand section 2 with two paragraphs about..."* then *"Expand section 3..."* and so on. After all sections are expanded, do a final pass: *"Review the full document* *for consistency in tone and smooth transitions between sections."* This produces a more cohesive document than asking ChatGPT to write it all at once.

The "bring your own draft" workflow: Write your first draft yourself, paste it into Canvas, and use ChatGPT as an editor. *"Read this draft. Don't change anything yet — just tell me what's strong and what needs work."* Get the assessment first. Then: *"Rework the introduction — it's weak"* and *"Tighten section 4 — it's too long."* This produces output that's unmistakably yours, with ChatGPT as a skilled editor rather than a ghostwriter.

The "code review" workflow: Paste your code into Canvas and ask ChatGPT to review it: *"Review this code for bugs, performance issues, and readability. Don't change anything — just comment on what you find."* Read the review. Then selectively ask ChatGPT to fix specific issues while leaving everything else untouched. This gives you a code review without the risk of ChatGPT rewriting code that works perfectly fine.

Canvas brings ChatGPT closer to being a true writing partner rather than just a response machine. For anyone who does substantial writing or coding, it's a feature worth building into your workflow.

We've now covered ChatGPT's creative tools. Part IV dives into the full range of productivity features — starting with vision and document analysis in Chapter 13.

Part IV: Productivity Tools

"The first rule of any technology used in a business is that automation applied to an efficient operation will magnify the efficiency."

— Bill Gates

Chapter 13: Vision — Images and Documents

ChatGPT can see. Upload a photo, screenshot, document, or handwritten note, and it can analyze, describe, extract information from, and answer questions about what it sees. This chapter covers the practical ways to use ChatGPT's vision capabilities.

How to Share Images

There are several ways to give ChatGPT something to look at:

- **Upload a file** – Click the attachment button and select an image or document from your device
- **Take a photo** – On mobile, use the camera button to snap a picture directly
- **Paste from clipboard** – On desktop, paste a screenshot with Ctrl+V / Cmd+V
- **Drag and drop** – Drag files directly into the chat window on desktop
- **Share from other apps** – On mobile, use the share sheet to send images to ChatGPT

You can upload multiple images in a single message, and you can mix images with text.

Photo Analysis

Upload any photo and ChatGPT can tell you about it:

[Upload a photo of a plant] "What kind of plant is this? Is it healthy? How should I care for it?"

[Upload a photo of a meal] "What dish is this? Estimate the calories and macronutrients."

[Upload a photo of a room] "How would you redesign this living room for a more modern look? Keep the existing furniture layout."

[Upload a photo of a stain] "What kind of stain is this on my shirt, and how do I remove it?"

[Upload a photo of a rash] "What might this be? Note: I know you're not a doctor — I'm asking for general information before I schedule an appointment."

ChatGPT's visual analysis is good at identification: plants, animals, foods, landmarks, artwork, products, and objects. It's less reliable for medical and diagnostic purposes — always follow up with a professional for health-related visual assessments.

Prompts that get the most out of photo analysis:

[Photo of a piece of furniture at a thrift store] "What style is this chair? What era is it from? Is it likely valuable or just old?"

[Photo of your car dashboard with a warning light] "What does this warning light mean? How urgent is it? What should I do?"

[Photo of a bug in your kitchen] "Identify this insect. Is it harmful? How do I get rid of it? Should I be concerned about an infestation?"

[Photo of a math problem on a whiteboard] "Solve this step by step."

The key to good photo analysis is asking specific questions rather than uploading without context. *"What is this?"* works, but *"What kind of plant is this, is it suitable for low-light indoor conditions, and how often should I water it?"* gets you much more useful output in a single response.

The honest take on photo accuracy: ChatGPT is good at identifying common things — popular houseplants, dog breeds, famous landmarks, common insects. It's less reliable for rare species, subtle distinctions (is this a chanterelle mushroom or a toxic look-alike?), and anything where the visual differences are small. For anything with safety implications — is this plant edible? is this snake venomous? is this skin condition serious? — verify with an expert. ChatGPT's identification is a starting point, not a definitive answer.

Document Analysis

This is one of the most practically useful vision features. Upload documents — PDFs, Word files, PowerPoint presentations, or photos of printed pages — and ChatGPT can:

Summarize: *[Upload a 30-page report] "Summarize the key findings and recommendations in five bullet points."*

Extract specific information: *[Upload a contract] "What is the termination clause? What are the payment terms?"*

Analyze: *[Upload financial statements] "Compare Q1 and Q2 performance. What are the main trends?"*

Convert: *[Upload a photo of a printed table] "Convert this table to CSV format."*

Translate: *[Upload a document in another language] "Translate this to English and summarize the main points."*

For long documents, GPT-5.4 significantly outperforms GPT-5.3 on comprehension and accuracy. If you're analyzing an important or complex document, switch to the more powerful model.

A document analysis workflow that saves hours:

Upload a contract or legal agreement and try these prompts in sequence: 1. *"Summarize this agreement in plain English. What am I agreeing to?"* 2. *"What are the key obligations on my side? List them as a checklist."* 3. *"Are there any unusual clauses, penalties, or automatic renewals I should know about?"* 4. *"What are the termination conditions? How much notice do I need to give?"* 5. *"If I were a lawyer reviewing this for a client, what would I flag as potential concerns?"*

This turns a 20-page contract you might skim (or skip) into a structured understanding of what you're signing. It doesn't replace legal advice for important contracts, but it makes you a far more informed party in any negotiation.

Screenshots and UI Analysis

Screenshots are one of the most versatile things you can share with ChatGPT:

Error messages: *[Screenshot of an error] "What does this error mean and how do I fix it?"*

Software help: *[Screenshot of an application] "How do I create a pivot table in this spreadsheet? I can see the data is in columns A through F."*

Design feedback: *[Screenshot of a website] "Review this landing page design. What would you improve for better conversion?"*

Comparison: *[Screenshots of two products] "Compare these two laptops based on the spec sheets shown."*

This is especially useful for tech support. Instead of describing an error message or a confusing interface, show ChatGPT what you're seeing.

The screenshot-as-context technique: Screenshots aren't just for errors. They're a fast way to provide context for any question. Instead of describing a complex Excel layout, screenshot it. Instead of explaining a Figma design, screenshot it. Instead of describing the format of a report you want replicated, screenshot one page. Visual context is faster and more accurate than verbal description, and ChatGPT interprets screenshots with remarkable precision.

Handwriting Recognition

ChatGPT can read handwritten text — notes, to-do lists, letters, whiteboard content, and even messy scribbles:

[Photo of handwritten meeting notes] "Transcribe these notes and organize them into a clean summary with action items."

[Photo of a whiteboard] "Transcribe everything on this whiteboard and organize it into a structured document."

[Photo of a handwritten recipe from grandma] "Transcribe this recipe and format it with ingredients list and numbered steps."

The accuracy depends on handwriting legibility, but ChatGPT handles a wide range of handwriting styles surprisingly well.

A time-saving workflow for handwritten notes: After every meeting, snap a photo of your handwritten notes, send it to ChatGPT, and ask: *"Transcribe these notes, organize them into sections, extract any action items, and format it as a clean summary I can share with the team."* This turns messy scribbles into a shareable document in about thirty seconds. Many people find this workflow so useful they go back to handwriting notes specifically because ChatGPT makes the digitization step effortless.

Business card scanning: Take a photo of a business card and ask: *"Extract the name, title, company, phone, email, and address from this card. Format it as a contact entry."* Quick, accurate, no manual typing.

Multimodal Conversations

You can mix images and text freely throughout a conversation:

1. Start with a text question about home renovation
2. Upload a photo of your kitchen
3. Ask for design suggestions based on the photo
4. Upload a floor plan
5. Ask ChatGPT to suggest a new layout
6. Take a photo of a paint swatch and ask how it would look

This fluid mixing of visual and text information is what makes ChatGPT's vision capabilities practical rather than novelty. You're not limited to one mode of communication.

A multimodal workflow that saves real time: You're shopping for a used car. Snap a photo of the listing sheet at the dealership. Upload it and ask: *"Extract all the key specs from this listing. Then search the web for reviews of this model and year. Is this a good car? What are the common problems? Is the price fair for this mileage?"* You've combined vision (reading the listing), data extraction (pulling specs), web search (finding reviews), and analysis (evaluating the deal) in a single conversation. A 30-minute research session compressed into 2 minutes.

Walkthrough: Extracting Data from a Receipt

Step 1: Take a photo of a receipt (or a pile of receipts).

Step 2: *"Read this receipt. Extract the store name, date, each line item with its price, subtotal, tax, and total. Format it as a table."*

Step 3: *"Now categorize each item: groceries, household supplies, or personal care."*

Step 4: *"Add this to a running spreadsheet format. I'll upload more receipts — keep a cumulative total by category."*

Upload your next receipt and say: *"Add this one to the same tracking."*

A workflow that would be tedious by hand — reading receipts, typing data, categorizing items — compressed into a quick photo-and-chat interaction.

Privacy Considerations

When uploading images and documents, keep in mind:

- Images are processed by OpenAI's servers
- On Free, Go, and Plus plans, uploaded content may be used for model training unless you've opted out in Data Controls
- Business and Enterprise plans exclude all uploaded content from training by default
- Don't upload documents containing sensitive personal information (Social Security numbers, medical records, financial account details) unless you're on a Business or Enterprise plan with appropriate protections
- Temporary Chat mode prevents uploaded images from being stored in your conversation history

Tips for Better Vision Results

Image quality matters. A blurry, poorly lit photo produces worse analysis than a clear one. For document analysis, make sure the text is sharp and readable. For photo identification, make sure the subject is clearly visible. A few seconds of repositioning saves you from uploading, getting an "I can't quite read that" response, and re-uploading.

Provide context with your image. Don't just upload a photo with no text. Tell ChatGPT what you want to know. *"What kind of plant is this?"* gets a better response than uploading a plant photo with no prompt, because ChatGPT knows you want identification rather than a general description.

Multiple images in one message. When comparing two things — two products, two designs, two documents — upload both images in the same message and ask for the comparison. ChatGPT can analyze them side by side: *"Here are screenshots of two laptop spec sheets. Which one is better for video editing? Explain the key differences."*

Vision capabilities transform ChatGPT from a text-only tool into something that can interact with the visual world around you. In the next chapter, we'll explore voice and audio — the other dimension that makes ChatGPT feel more like a conversation partner than a chatbot.

Chapter 14: Voice and Audio

ChatGPT can talk. Not in a robotic, text-to-speech way — in a natural, conversational, surprisingly human way. Advanced Voice Mode transforms ChatGPT from something you type at into something you talk with.

Advanced Voice Mode

Advanced Voice Mode is available on Plus, Pro, and Business plans. To use it, tap the voice icon (the waveform button) in the ChatGPT app.

Once activated, you're in a real-time spoken conversation. You talk, ChatGPT listens, thinks, and responds aloud. The voice is natural — it has inflection, pacing, and appropriate emotional tone. It can express enthusiasm, concern, thoughtfulness, and humor.

What makes it remarkable: - Near-zero latency — responses come almost immediately - You can interrupt mid-sentence, just like a real conversation - It understands context, tone, and implied meaning in your voice - It can maintain long, multi-topic conversations - It works in dozens of languages

What it feels like: The first time you use Advanced Voice Mode, it will probably surprise you. The voice is natural enough that you forget, for a moment, you're talking to software. It laughs (appropriately), pauses to think, adjusts its pace to match yours, and sounds engaged. This isn't the stilted, robotic voice assistant experience you might be expecting. For many people, voice mode is the feature that changes their relationship with ChatGPT entirely — from a tool they use to something closer to a conversation partner.

The honest caveat: Voice mode is impressive but not perfect. It occasionally misinterprets words in noisy environments, can go on tangents if you're not clear, and sometimes gives longer responses than you need. Quality varies by context — excellent on a quiet walk with AirPods, less reliable on a busy street or in a car with the windows down.

When to Use Voice

Voice mode isn't just a novelty — there are situations where it's genuinely the best way to use ChatGPT:

Hands-free situations. Cooking, driving, exercising, or any time your hands are occupied.

Thinking out loud. Some people process ideas better by talking than typing. Voice mode lets you brainstorm verbally.

Language practice. Spoken conversation in a language you're learning is dramatically more effective than reading and writing exercises alone. ChatGPT is a patient, always-available conversation partner.

Quick questions. When pulling out your phone and typing feels like too much friction, just ask aloud.

Accessibility. For users who have difficulty typing due to physical limitations, voice mode provides full access to ChatGPT's capabilities.

Companionship and emotional processing. Many people use voice mode to talk through their day, process feelings, or have a thoughtful conversation. ChatGPT is empathetic in its responses, but remember it's not a therapist (see Chapter 30).

Scenarios where voice mode is the clear winner: You're cooking and don't know how long to roast a chicken at 375 — ask aloud without washing your hands. You're driving and need to brainstorm a response to an email — talk it through hands-free. You're exercising and want to understand a concept — turn your workout into a learning session. You're in bed and don't want to look at a screen — have a voice conversation in the dark. Voice mode excels in all the moments typing isn't practical or desirable.

Customizable Personalities

ChatGPT includes several personality options that change how it interacts. These are currently available in text chat, with voice support coming later:

- **Default** — Balanced, helpful, conversational

- **Cynic** — Dry, skeptical, slightly sardonic
- **Robot** — Precise, analytical, matter-of-fact
- **Listener** — Warm, empathetic, patient
- **Nerd** — Enthusiastic, detailed, excited about knowledge

These personalities affect tone and conversational style, not the underlying intelligence. A response from "Nerd" contains the same information as one from "Cynic" — it's just delivered differently.

Choose a personality that matches how you like to interact. You can switch between them at any time.

Voice on Different Platforms

Voice mode works across platforms with some variation:

Mobile (iOS and Android): The best voice experience. Low latency, high quality, always available.

Web (chat.com): Voice mode works in the browser on supported devices.

Windows desktop app: Full voice support.

macOS: Advanced Voice Mode was removed from the macOS desktop app in January 2026. For voice conversations on Mac, use chat.com in your browser, or use the iOS app on an iPhone or iPad.

Real-Time Translation

One of voice mode's most practical applications is live translation. You can have a three-way conversation where:

1. You speak in English
2. ChatGPT translates to another language and speaks it aloud
3. The other person responds in their language
4. ChatGPT translates back to English

This works in real time, making it useful for travel, business meetings with international partners, or any situation where you need to communicate across a language barrier.

"I need you to be my translator. I'm going to speak in English, and I need you to translate everything I say into Mandarin Chinese. When someone responds in Mandarin, translate it back to English for me."

How well does real-time translation actually work? For common languages (Spanish, French, German, Mandarin, Japanese), it works well. Translations are natural-sounding and conversationally appropriate — not the stilted phrasing of Google Translate. For less common languages, quality varies. The main limitation is speed in three-way conversations: there's a natural delay as ChatGPT processes and translates each statement, which can make the rhythm feel slightly off. But for travelers ordering food, asking directions, or having basic conversations, it's practical — far better than frantically typing into a translation app.

A real-world travel scenario: You're at a train station in Japan and need to ask the attendant about the right platform. Open voice mode, tell ChatGPT to be your translator, hold the phone between you, and have a conversation. ChatGPT translates your English to Japanese and their Japanese to English, in real time. Not perfect, but it turns an impossible communication barrier into a functional conversation.

Tips for Better Voice Conversations

Speak naturally. You don't need to talk in a special way. Use your normal speaking voice, normal pace, and normal vocabulary.

Be okay with interrupting. If ChatGPT is going in the wrong direction, just start talking. It will stop and listen.

Ask it to be concise. Voice responses can be long. If you want shorter answers: *"Keep your responses brief — a few sentences max."*

Use it for back-and-forth. Voice mode excels at iterative conversations where you're building on ideas. It's less ideal for tasks where you need formatted output (tables, code, specific documents) — for those, switch to text.

Remember it can see too. On mobile, you can use voice mode while also sharing your camera. Point your phone at something and ask about it verbally: *"What kind of tree is this?"* or *"Can you read this sign for me?"*

Voice vs. Text: Which to Use When

Situation	Better Mode
Need formatted output (tables, code, lists)	Text
Hands are free, at a desk	Text or voice — your preference
Driving, cooking, exercising	Voice
Brainstorming ideas	Voice
Writing a document	Text (with Canvas)
Language practice	Voice
Quick factual question	Voice
Complex multi-step task	Text
Emotional conversation	Voice
Need to share/save the output	Text

There's no wrong answer. Many people switch between voice and text throughout the day depending on context. The key insight: voice mode isn't a lesser version of ChatGPT — it's the same intelligence, accessed differently.

A common pattern users discover: Start the day with voice mode (catching up while getting ready), switch to text during focused work (where you need formatted output), and return to voice in the evening (processing the day, planning tomorrow, or just talking). ChatGPT's multimodal nature means you don't have to choose — use whichever fits the moment.

Voice mode for processing your thinking: One of the most underappreciated uses of voice mode is talking through complex decisions or creative challenges. Many people think more clearly when they talk than when they type. Voice mode gives you an active listener that can respond, ask clarifying questions, and offer perspectives — all while you pace around your living room working through a thorny problem. Thinking out loud, with a thoughtful conversation partner instead of an empty room.

Walkthrough: Voice Mode for Language Practice

One of voice mode's strongest practical applications:

You: *"I want to practice conversational Spanish. Speak to me in Spanish at a beginner level. If I make a grammar mistake, gently correct me in English, then continue in Spanish. Let's start — ask me about my day."*

ChatGPT: Greets you in simple Spanish and asks about your day.

You: Respond in your best Spanish, stumbling through verb conjugations.

ChatGPT: Responds naturally, slips in a gentle correction ("Just a small note — 'fui' not 'fue' when talking about yourself"), then continues the conversation.

This works for any language ChatGPT supports. The experience is close to having a patient conversation partner — one who never tires, never judges, and adapts to your exact level.

Audio Input Beyond Voice

While Advanced Voice Mode is the headline feature, ChatGPT can also work with audio files:

Meeting recordings. Upload a recording of a meeting and ask ChatGPT to transcribe and summarize it: *"Transcribe this audio and identify the key decisions, action items, and open questions."*

Podcast analysis. Upload a podcast episode and ask: *"Summarize this podcast episode. What were the three main topics discussed? What were the most interesting insights?"*

Music and audio identification. While not its strongest capability, ChatGPT can sometimes identify songs, instruments, and musical styles from audio clips.

The practical limitation: Audio file processing works best with clear speech in common languages. Background noise, overlapping speakers, and heavy accents reduce accuracy. For high-quality transcription of important recordings (legal proceedings, medical consultations, formal interviews), use a dedicated transcription service and then bring the text to ChatGPT for analysis.

In the next chapter, we'll explore ChatGPT's data analysis capabilities — how it can process spreadsheets, create visualizations, and help you make sense of numbers.

Chapter 15: Code Interpreter and Data Analysis

You don't need to know how to code or use complex spreadsheet formulas to do data analysis. ChatGPT's Code Interpreter lets you upload files, analyze data, create visualizations, and download results — all through conversation.

What Code Interpreter Does

When you upload a data file or ask ChatGPT to perform calculations, it writes and executes Python code behind the scenes. You don't see the code (unless you ask to) — you just see the results: charts, tables, cleaned data, calculations, and downloadable files.

This means ChatGPT can: - Process CSV, Excel, JSON, and other data files - Create charts and visualizations - Perform statistical analysis - Clean and transform data - Run complex calculations - Generate new files for you to download

Uploading and Analyzing Data

Click the attachment button and upload your file, then tell ChatGPT what you want:

[Upload sales.csv] "Analyze this sales data. What are the key trends? Which products are performing best?"

[Upload survey_results.xlsx] "Summarize the results of this survey. Show me the distribution of responses for each question."

[Upload expenses.csv] "Categorize these expenses and tell me where I'm spending the most. Create a pie chart."

ChatGPT will read the file, understand its structure, and produce the analysis you asked for. If the data has issues (missing values, inconsistent formatting, duplicates), it will often identify and handle them automatically.

The "first look" prompt that saves time: Before diving into specific analysis, start with an overview: *"Describe this dataset. How many rows and columns? What are the column names and data types? Are there any missing values, duplicates, or obvious data quality issues?"* This gives you a foundation and often reveals problems (wrong date formats, inconsistent categories, missing data) before they corrupt your analysis. The data equivalent of checking your ingredients before cooking.

What formats work best: CSV files are the most reliable — simple, universal, no formatting surprises. Excel files work too, though complex spreadsheets with multiple sheets, pivot tables, and conditional formatting may lose some of that complexity in processing. If you have data in Google Sheets, export it as CSV before uploading. JSON files work for structured data. If your data is in an unusual format, paste it directly into the chat — ChatGPT can often parse text-based data that isn't in a standard file format.

Creating Visualizations

Ask for any type of chart and ChatGPT will create it:

- **Bar charts:** *"Show monthly revenue as a bar chart."*
- **Line charts:** *"Plot the trend of customer signups over time."*
- **Pie charts:** *"Show the breakdown of expenses by category."*
- **Scatter plots:** *"Plot the correlation between marketing spend and revenue."*
- **Histograms:** *"Show the distribution of customer ages."*
- **Heatmaps:** *"Create a heatmap of sales by region and product."*

You can customize charts through follow-up prompts:

"Make the colors match our brand (blue and orange)." "Add data labels to each bar." "Make the font larger — this is for a presentation." "Change it to a horizontal bar chart and sort by value."

Charts can be downloaded as images to use in presentations, reports, or documents.

Making charts presentation-ready: The default charts ChatGPT produces are functional but plain. A few follow-up prompts make them polished enough for a client presentation or board meeting. Try these in sequence: *"Increase the font size — this will be projected on a screen"* then *"Use our brand colors: dark blue (#1E3A5F) and orange (#FF6B35)"* then *"Remove the grid lines and add a clean border"* then *"Add a descriptive title and subtitle."* Four prompts turn a default matplotlib chart into something that looks intentionally designed.

Spreadsheet Creation and Editing

GPT-5.4 introduced significantly improved spreadsheet capabilities. ChatGPT can:

Create spreadsheets from scratch: *"Create a budget spreadsheet for a small business. Include categories for revenue, fixed costs, variable costs, and profit. Include formulas that calculate totals and margins."*

Build templates: *"Create a project tracking spreadsheet with columns for task name, owner, status, priority, due date, and notes. Add conditional formatting rules."*

Convert formats: *"I have data in this JSON file. Convert it to a clean Excel spreadsheet with proper column headers."*

"Take this PDF table and convert it into an editable spreadsheet."

Write formulas: *"Write an Excel formula that calculates the running average of the last 12 months of data in column B."*

"I need a VLOOKUP that matches customer IDs in Sheet 1 with order totals in Sheet 2."

Data Cleaning

Real-world data is messy. ChatGPT can clean it up:

"This dataset has inconsistent date formats — some are MM/DD/YYYY and some are DD-MM-YYYY. Standardize them all to YYYY-MM-DD."

"Remove duplicate rows based on the email column, keeping the most recent entry."

"The 'state' column has a mix of full names and abbreviations. Convert everything to two-letter abbreviations."

"Fill in missing values in the 'category' column based on the product name patterns."

Practical Examples

Personal finance: *[Upload bank statement CSV] "Categorize all my transactions for the last three months. Show me a breakdown of spending by category, and identify my top 5 unnecessary expenses."*

Business metrics: *[Upload monthly data] "Calculate month-over-month growth rates, create a 3-month rolling average, and project the next quarter based on the current trend."*

Academic research: *[Upload survey data] "Run a basic statistical analysis on this survey data. Calculate mean, median, standard deviation for each numeric question. Test for significant differences between the two groups."*

Real estate: *"Here's a list of 20 apartments I'm considering [paste data]. Create a scoring matrix that weighs price (40%), commute time (30%), size (20%), and amenities (10%). Rank them."*

Downloading Results

After ChatGPT processes your data, you can download the results. It can generate:

- Cleaned and transformed data files (CSV, Excel)
- Charts and visualizations (PNG, SVG)
- Reports (formatted text or PDF)
- New spreadsheets with formulas

Look for the download link in ChatGPT's response, or ask: *"Give me a downloadable Excel file with this analysis."*

Walkthrough: Analyzing a Sales Spreadsheet

Step 1: Upload your sales data file.

Step 2: *"Give me an overview of this data. How many records are there? What's the date range? What columns do we have?"*

Step 3: *"Show me total revenue by month as a line chart. Highlight any months with significant changes."*

Step 4: *"Which product categories are growing fastest? Show me year-over-year growth rates."*

Step 5: *"Create a summary dashboard with four charts: monthly revenue trend, top 10 products by revenue, revenue by region, and average order value over time."*

Step 6: *"Write up a brief analysis of the key findings — three paragraphs I can paste into a report."*

Step 7: *"Package everything into a downloadable Excel file with the raw data on one tab, the summary statistics on another, and the charts on a third."*

You just did what used to require an analyst with Excel and Python skills, and you did it in a conversation.

Tips for Better Data Analysis

Describe your goal, not just your data. Instead of *"Analyze this spreadsheet,"* try *"I need to understand which marketing channels are driving the most revenue per dollar spent."* The goal shapes the analysis.

Ask for the methodology. If you're presenting the results to others, ask: *"Explain how you calculated this, so I can describe the methodology."*

Verify surprising results. If ChatGPT finds something unexpected in your data, ask it to double-check: *"That growth rate seems high. Can you verify the calculation and show me the raw numbers?"*

Iterate on visualizations. The first chart is rarely perfect. Refine colors, labels, and layout through follow-ups until it's presentation-ready.

Watch for silent assumptions. When ChatGPT analyzes your data, it makes assumptions about date formats, how to handle missing values, and what "average" means (mean vs. median). For serious analysis, ask: *"What* *assumptions did you make? How did you handle missing values and outliers?"* Understanding the assumptions prevents you from presenting conclusions that are technically correct but practically misleading.

When to use Code Interpreter vs. asking ChatGPT to reason about numbers: For simple comparisons and estimates, regular ChatGPT is fine. For anything involving actual calculations — percentages, growth rates, statistical tests, financial projections — ask it to use Code Interpreter. *"Use Python to calculate this"* or uploading a data file triggers Code Interpreter automatically. The difference matters because Code Interpreter runs actual code with precise arithmetic, while ChatGPT's natural reasoning can make arithmetic errors on multi-step calculations.

A Note on Codex

You may see references to *Codex* in ChatGPT — particularly on Pro plans and in student-facing features. Codex is OpenAI's separate agentic coding tool, designed for developers who need ChatGPT to work autonomously on codebases: writing code, running tests, and making changes across multiple files.

Codex is distinct from Code Interpreter. Code Interpreter runs Python within your ChatGPT conversation to analyze data and produce results. Codex operates more like Agent Mode for software development — it takes a task description and works through it independently, writing and testing code in a sandboxed environment.

If you're not a developer, you can safely ignore Codex. If you are, it's worth exploring — and verified university students in the United States and Canada can claim $100 in Codex credits through OpenAI's student program.

What Code Interpreter Can't Do

It can't access the internet. Code Interpreter runs in a sandboxed environment without web access. It works only with data you've uploaded or that it generates itself. If you need to combine web data with analysis, do the web search first, then switch to Code Interpreter.

It has session limits. The computing environment resets between conversations. If you upload data and create an analysis, the computed results live only within that conversation. To reference the analysis later, download the output files. Starting a new conversation means re-uploading.

Complex visualizations have limits. ChatGPT runs Python's matplotlib and related libraries behind the scenes. Highly interactive visualizations (hover effects, clickable elements, animated dashboards) aren't possible. For static charts in presentations and reports, it's excellent. For interactive dashboards, use Tableau or Power BI — and use ChatGPT to prep the data for those tools.

Large files can be slow. Files over a few hundred thousand rows may take a long time to process or hit memory limits. For very large datasets, pre-filter your data before uploading. You don't need to upload a 5-million-row database to analyze last quarter's sales — export just the rows you need.

In the next chapter, we'll look at how ChatGPT searches the web to bring you current, cited information.

Chapter 16: Web Search

ChatGPT can search the internet, read web pages, and synthesize what it finds into clear answers with citations. This bridges the gap between ChatGPT's training data (which has a knowledge cutoff) and the real-time web.

How ChatGPT Search Works

When you ask a question that requires current information, ChatGPT:

1. Formulates search queries based on your question
2. Searches the web
3. Reads relevant pages from the results
4. Synthesizes the information
5. Presents an answer with clickable citations

On paid plans, this often happens automatically — ChatGPT detects when your question needs current information and searches without being asked. You can also request it explicitly:

"Search the web and find the latest reviews of the Samsung Galaxy S26." "What happened in the stock market today?" "Find me the current schedule for Amtrak trains from New York to Boston."

When ChatGPT Searches vs. Uses Training Data

ChatGPT uses its training data when: - The question is about well-established knowledge (how things work, definitions, concepts) - The answer hasn't changed recently - You're asking for creative output, analysis, or advice

ChatGPT searches the web when: - The question involves current events, recent developments, or time-sensitive information - You explicitly ask it to search - The information is likely to have changed since its training data was collected - You ask about specific products, prices, or availability

If you're unsure whether ChatGPT is using current information, ask: *"Is this based on your training data or a web search? If it's training data, please search for the latest information."*

How to tell if ChatGPT searched the web: When ChatGPT searches, you'll see a visual indicator — usually a "Searching..." or "Browsing..." status message before the response. The response will also include numbered citations with clickable links to the source pages. No citations means the response is coming from training data, not the live web. This distinction matters because training data can be months old; web search results are current.

A subtle trap to avoid: ChatGPT can mix training data and web search results in the same response without flagging which claims come from which source. Ask about a topic where some information is timeless (how photosynthesis works) and some is time-sensitive (the latest research on plant gene editing), and the response may blend both seamlessly. The timeless parts are reliable from training data; the time-sensitive parts need citations. When accuracy matters, check that the specific claims you care about have citations attached.

Citations and Verification

When ChatGPT searches the web, it provides citations — numbered references linked to the source pages. These are crucial:

- **Click the citations** to verify the information comes from a reliable source
- **Check the date** of the source — even web search can surface outdated pages
- **Read the original** for context that ChatGPT may have summarized too aggressively
- **Cross-reference** important claims across multiple sources

Citations transform ChatGPT from a black box into a verifiable research tool. Always use them.

ChatGPT Search vs. Google

ChatGPT search and traditional search engines serve different purposes:

ChatGPT search is better for: - Getting a synthesized answer instead of a list of links - Complex questions that span multiple sources - Follow-up questions and refinement - Comparative research ("compare X and Y based on recent reviews")

Google/traditional search is better for: - Finding a specific website or page - Browsing multiple sources to form your own opinion - Local search (nearby restaurants, stores, services) - Shopping and price comparison - Image and video search - Discovering sources you didn't know existed

The practical approach: Use ChatGPT search when you want an answer. Use Google when you want to explore. Many people use both in the same research session — ChatGPT to quickly understand a topic, then Google to go deeper on specific aspects.

Where ChatGPT search saves time: Comparison questions. Try: *"Search the web and compare the current pricing, features, and user reviews of Notion, Monday.com, and Asana for a team of 10."* Manually, you'd visit three websites, navigate to their pricing pages, cross-reference review sites, and compile the information yourself. ChatGPT does all of that and delivers a synthesized comparison in one response. For any "compare X, Y, and Z" question, ChatGPT search beats traditional search by a wide margin.

Where traditional search still wins: Anything visual (what does this product look like?), anything local (restaurants near me right now), and anything where you want to browse and evaluate sources yourself. ChatGPT gives you its synthesis; Google gives you the raw materials to form your own judgment. Both have their place.

Tips for Better Search Results

Be specific about what you want: Instead of *"Tell me about electric cars"*, try *"What are the top-rated electric SUVs under $50,000 in 2026? Compare range, price, and charging speed."*

Specify recency when it matters: *"Find articles from the last month about..."* or *"What's the latest news about..."*

Ask for multiple sources: *"Search for this and provide at least three different sources with links."*

Ask for primary sources: *"Find the original study, not just articles about the study. I want the peer-reviewed paper or the official report, not a news summary of it."*

Combine search with analysis: *"Search for the current mortgage rates from major lenders, then help me calculate monthly payments on a $400K loan at each rate."*

Use follow-up searches to go deeper: After an initial search, drill down: *"You mentioned that Company X just raised a Series C round. Search for the details — how much did they raise, who led the round, and what are they planning to use it for?"* ChatGPT can chain searches, moving from broad to specific across multiple rounds.

Ask for the contrarian view: *"Search the web for arguments against intermittent fasting. I've already read the positive research — I want to see the criticisms and limitations."* This counters confirmation bias by explicitly requesting information that challenges the prevailing narrative.

Limitations of ChatGPT Search

ChatGPT search is powerful, but it has real constraints:

It can't access paywalled content. Articles behind paywalls (New York Times, Wall Street Journal, academic journals) are typically inaccessible. ChatGPT may see the headline and summary but not the full text.

It can't see real-time data. Stock prices, live sports scores, and other real-time feeds aren't available through standard web search. It searches the web like a person would, which means a slight delay.

It may not find niche sources. Like any search engine, ChatGPT's search favors well-known, high-ranking pages. Obscure forums, small blogs, or specialized databases may not surface.

Citation quality varies. Not all cited sources are authoritative. A citation proves ChatGPT read a page — not that the page is reliable. Evaluate the source, not just the claim.

The honest assessment of ChatGPT search quality: It's strong for general information gathering and comparison shopping. It's weaker on niche topics where the best sources are specialized forums, academic databases, or expert blogs that don't rank highly. If you're researching something obscure — a rare medical condition, an unusual historical event, a highly technical engineering problem — ChatGPT search may surface only surface-level sources. In those cases, use ChatGPT to identify key terms and concepts, then run targeted searches on specialized platforms (Google Scholar for academic papers, Reddit for community knowledge, Stack Overflow for programming questions).

Walkthrough: Researching a Purchase Decision

You: *"I'm considering buying an electric vehicle. Search the web for the best-rated EVs under $45,000 in 2026. Focus on range, charging speed, and real-owner satisfaction, not just expert reviews."*

ChatGPT: [Searches multiple sources, compiles a comparison with citations]

You: *"Now compare the top three on total cost of ownership over 5 years, including estimated electricity costs, maintenance, and insurance."*

You: *"Are there any federal or state incentives available in Colorado for these vehicles?"*

You: *"Based on everything, which one would you recommend for someone who drives 60 miles per day and has a garage for home charging?"*

In four messages, you've done research that would have taken an hour of browsing, reading reviews, checking government incentive pages, and running cost calculations.

Getting the Most From Search-Assisted Conversations

The most powerful use of ChatGPT search isn't asking a single question — it's combining search with ChatGPT's analytical capabilities in a multi-step conversation.

Step 1: Ask ChatGPT to search for raw information: *"Search for the latest data on remote work trends in 2026."*

Step 2: Ask for analysis: *"Based on what you found, what are the three most significant trends? Which ones are most relevant for a company considering a hybrid work policy?"*

Step 3: Ask for application: *"Draft a memo to my leadership team recommending a hybrid work policy based on these trends. Cite the specific data you found."*

This three-step pattern — gather, analyze, apply — is where ChatGPT search goes from "better Google" to a real research and drafting workflow. Each step builds on the last, and the final output is grounded in current data with citations.

A note on search freshness: ChatGPT search results are only as current as the web pages it finds. For fast-moving topics — stock prices, election results, breaking news — the information may be minutes or hours old by the time you see it. For most purposes this is fine, but don't rely on ChatGPT search for time-critical decisions that require the latest data. For those, go to the primary source directly.

Search as a Fact-Checking Tool

One of the most valuable uses of web search is verifying ChatGPT's own claims. If ChatGPT tells you something in a regular (non-search) response and you want to confirm it, follow up: *"Search the web and verify that claim."* This two-step pattern — get an answer from training data, then verify via search — gives you the speed of ChatGPT's internal knowledge with the accuracy of sourced, current information.

A practical example: You ask ChatGPT about the side effects of a medication. It gives you a list based on training data. You follow up: *"Search the web for the current prescribing information for this medication and confirm these side effects."* Now you have verified, sourced information — and you'll quickly see if the training data was outdated or incomplete.

The verify-via-search approach matters most for medical information, financial data, legal details, and any other domain where accuracy is critical and information changes frequently.

Web search makes ChatGPT a real-time research tool. But for complex research tasks, Deep Research (covered in Chapter 7) goes much deeper — reading dozens of sources and producing structured reports with comprehensive citations.

Next up: Agent Mode — where ChatGPT doesn't just search and analyze, but takes action on your behalf.

Part V: Automation and Customization

"I visualise a time when we will be to robots what dogs are to humans, and I'm rooting for the machines."

— Claude Shannon

Chapter 17: Agent Mode

Agent Mode is the most consequential feature ChatGPT has added since its launch. Instead of just answering questions and generating text, Agent Mode lets ChatGPT take action — completing tasks on your behalf using a virtual computer, browser, and suite of tools.

This is where ChatGPT shifts from assistant to agent.

What Agent Mode Is

When you activate Agent Mode, ChatGPT gets access to:

- **A visual browser** — It can navigate websites, click buttons, fill forms, and interact with web pages just like you would
- **A text-based browser** — For simpler web queries and data retrieval
- **A terminal** — It can run commands and execute code
- **File handling** — It can create, read, and modify files
- **API access** — It can interact with web services directly
- **Connectors** — It can read (not modify) data from services like Gmail and Google Drive

ChatGPT uses these tools autonomously, planning a sequence of steps and executing them to complete your request.

What this looks like in practice: When you give Agent Mode a task, you can watch it work in real time. It opens a browser, navigates to a website, scrolls through content, clicks links, reads pages, and takes notes — just like you would. The difference is that it does this methodically across multiple sites, extracting and organizing information as it goes. Watching it work for the first time is both impressive and slightly eerie — it's like watching someone use your computer at high speed, making decisions you would have made yourself.

The shift: Regular ChatGPT generates text from what it already knows. Agent Mode takes actions in the world to accomplish goals. It's the difference between asking someone to tell you what's on a website and asking them to go look and report back. Subtle distinction, large practical implications.

How to Use It

Agent Mode is available to Plus, Pro, and Business users. To activate it:

1. Open any conversation
2. Look for the tools dropdown in the composer area
3. Select "Agent Mode"
4. Describe the task you want completed

Or simply describe an agentic task and ChatGPT may suggest switching to Agent Mode automatically.

What Agent Mode Can Do

Research and analysis: *"Research the top five competitors in the project management space. Visit their websites, compare their pricing pages, and create a comparison spreadsheet."*

Form filling and applications: *"Fill out this conference registration form. Here are my details: [provide information]. Submit it when ready."*

Online tasks: *"Find the best-reviewed Italian restaurant near downtown Portland that's open tonight and has availability for four people."*

Data gathering: *"Go to [government website] and find the latest published economic data for [specific metric]. Download the dataset."*

Booking and scheduling: *"Find available flights from Chicago to Miami on March 15, returning March 19. Show me options under $400."*

Automating workflows: *"Visit these five websites, find their contact email addresses, and compile them into a spreadsheet."*

Tasks typically take 5 to 30 minutes depending on complexity. ChatGPT works through them methodically, and you can watch the progress in real time.

Practical prompts to try yourself:

"Go to the websites of three local electricians in [your city]. For each, find their services, customer reviews, and whether they list pricing. Create a comparison table with phone numbers."

"Visit the U.S. Bureau of Labor Statistics website and find the most recent unemployment rate, CPI data, and job growth figures. Compile them into a brief economic snapshot."

"Research the return policies at Amazon, Best Buy, and Target for electronics. How many days do I have? Are there restocking fees? Can I return opened items? Compare them."

Each task involves visiting multiple websites, navigating different site structures, finding specific information, and organizing it. Manually, that's 20–45 minutes. Agent Mode does it in 5–15, and the output is structured and ready to use.

The Collaborative Workflow

Agent Mode isn't a fire-and-forget system. It's designed for collaboration:

Permission requests. Before consequential actions — submitting a form, making a purchase, sending a message — ChatGPT asks for your permission. You stay in control.

Interruption. You can interrupt at any time to clarify instructions, change direction, or stop the task. It picks up where it left off with your new information.

Taking over the browser. If ChatGPT hits something it can't handle (a CAPTCHA, a complex login flow, a decision it needs your input on), you can take over the browser directly, handle the obstacle, and hand control back.

Iterative refinement. After a task completes, you can ask for changes: *"Good, but also add pricing information to the spreadsheet."*

Safety and Control

OpenAI has built several safety measures into Agent Mode:

- ChatGPT requests permission before consequential actions
- You can see what ChatGPT is doing at all times
- You can interrupt, redirect, or stop any task
- The system won't perform financial transactions without explicit confirmation

- Login credentials are handled through your browser session, not shared with the model

Best practices: - Don't share passwords directly in the chat — log into services in the browser session yourself - Review any forms or submissions before approving them - Start with simple tasks to build trust and understanding of how Agent Mode works - Be specific about what you want done and what you don't want done

When to Use Agent Mode vs. Regular Chat

Task	Mode
Answer a question	Regular chat
Write a document	Regular chat or Canvas
Research that requires browsing multiple sites	Agent Mode
Fill out forms online	Agent Mode
Compare products across websites	Agent Mode
Tasks with multiple sequential steps	Agent Mode
Quick creative or analytical tasks	Regular chat
Tasks requiring real-time web interaction	Agent Mode

The key distinction: if the task requires ChatGPT to *do things on the web* rather than just *generate text*, Agent Mode is the right choice.

Practical Tips

Be specific about the outcome. Rather than *"Research competitors,"* try *"Visit the websites of [Company A], [Company B], and [Company C]. For each, find their pricing, key features, and target market. Compile this into a comparison table."*

Provide context. If ChatGPT needs to navigate a specific website, tell it what you know about the site structure: *"The pricing information is usually under the 'Solutions' menu."*

Break complex tasks into stages. For very large tasks, give ChatGPT one stage at a time rather than everything at once. This lets you review and adjust between stages.

Save the results. Agent Mode outputs (spreadsheets, documents, data) can be downloaded. Save anything important — the results live in the conversation but aren't automatically stored elsewhere.

When Agent Mode Struggles

Agent Mode isn't infallible. Common friction points:

- **CAPTCHAs and anti-bot measures.** Some websites detect automated browsing and block it. You may need to take over the browser to solve a CAPTCHA.
- **Complex login flows.** Multi-factor authentication, unusual login pages, and SSO redirects can confuse the agent. Log in yourself first, then hand control back.
- **Dynamic web pages.** Sites with heavy JavaScript, constantly loading content, or unusual layouts can be harder for the agent to navigate reliably.
- **Ambiguous tasks.** If your instructions are vague, Agent Mode may make assumptions you didn't intend. Be specific about what "done" looks like.

When something goes wrong, you'll see the agent's actions in real time. You can interrupt, correct course, and let it continue — or take over and finish manually.

The honest assessment of Agent Mode reliability: On straightforward tasks and well-structured websites (government data portals, major retailer sites, popular web apps), Agent Mode is generally reliable, though far from infallible. On tasks with complex site navigation, login flows, or heavily dynamic pages, the success rate drops. The pattern is predictable: the more a site looks and behaves like a standard web page, the better Agent Mode handles it. The more it relies on custom JavaScript frameworks, pop-ups, and non-standard interactions, the more likely Agent Mode is to get confused.

A strategy for reliability: Break complex multi-site tasks into single-site tasks. Instead of *"Visit these five sites and compile..."*, try *"Visit [Site 1] and find [specific information]"* as a first task. Review the results, then send it to the next site. Checkpoints between steps prevent a failure on one site from derailing the entire task.

When to skip Agent Mode and just do it yourself: If the task takes you under five minutes manually and involves logging into a site (email, banking, internal tools), doing it yourself is usually faster. Agent Mode's strength is in tasks that are tedious because of their breadth (many sites, many data points) or repetition (the same action across many pages), not in quick tasks that require authentication.

Walkthrough: Competitive Research with Agent Mode

Let's walk through a real-world Agent Mode task from start to finish.

You: *"I need to research our top three competitors: [Company A], [Company B], and [Company C]. For each one, visit their website and find: (1) their pricing plans, (2) the key features they promote on their homepage, (3) any customer testimonials or case studies they feature, and (4) their latest blog post or press release. Compile everything into a comparison spreadsheet."*

What happens next: Agent Mode opens a browser and systematically visits each competitor's site. You can watch it navigate — it goes to the pricing page, reads the plan details, moves to the homepage to identify featured content, then finds the blog or press room. For each site, it extracts the relevant information and takes notes.

The result: After 10–20 minutes, you receive a structured spreadsheet comparing all three competitors across the dimensions you specified. The data is current (pulled from live websites), organized, and ready to share.

What this replaced: Manually visiting three websites, navigating multiple pages on each, taking notes, organizing them into a spreadsheet, and formatting it for presentation. Easily 60–90 minutes of tedious work.

The practical caveat: Agent Mode may miss information buried deep in a site or behind an unusual navigation pattern. After receiving the results, do a quick sanity check by visiting the most important pages yourself. Treat the output as a solid first draft, not a guaranteed complete picture.

Agent Mode represents a real shift in what AI assistants can do. It's early days, and it will get more capable over time. But even now, it saves hours on tasks involving repetitive browsing, data gathering, and form filling.

Next, we'll look at Tasks and automation — how to make ChatGPT do things on a schedule without you having to ask.

Chapter 18: Tasks, Scheduling, and Automation

ChatGPT can do things for you even when you're not actively using it. Tasks let you schedule actions, set reminders, and build automated workflows that run on their own.

Scheduled Tasks

You can ask ChatGPT to perform actions at specific times or on a recurring schedule:

"Remind me every Monday morning to submit my weekly timesheet."

"Every Friday at 3 PM, search the web for the latest news about [topic] and send me a summary."

"Check the weather for my area every morning at 7 AM and let me know if I need an umbrella."

ChatGPT will confirm the schedule, and the tasks will run automatically. You'll receive notifications when tasks complete.

What scheduled tasks look like: When you set up a task, ChatGPT shows a confirmation card summarizing what it will do, when, and how often. You can approve, modify, or cancel it right there. When the task runs, you get a notification (on mobile) or see the result in your conversation history (on web). The output is typically a brief message or summary — think of it as an automated update rather than a full conversation.

Good first tasks to try:

"Every weekday morning at 7:30 AM, give me a brief summary of the top three news stories from today."

"Every Sunday at 5 PM, remind me to review my calendar for the upcoming week and flag any meetings I need to prepare for."

"On the first of every month, remind me to check my credit card statements for any charges I don't recognize."

Start simple. Once you see how tasks work and build trust in the system, you can create more complex automated workflows.

Proactive Tasks

Beyond scheduled tasks, ChatGPT can proactively monitor things and alert you:

"Watch for price drops on [specific product] and let me know if it goes below $500."

"Monitor [news topic] and alert me if there are any significant developments."

"Check my calendar and remind me about upcoming deadlines."

The scope of proactive tasks depends on your plan tier and the connectors you've enabled.

The honest take on proactive tasks: This feature is still maturing. Price monitoring and news alerts work reasonably well for popular products and major topics. Niche monitoring — tracking a specific regulatory filing, watching an obscure product for updates, or monitoring a low-traffic website — is less reliable. Set expectations accordingly: think of proactive tasks as a convenient reminder service, not a comprehensive monitoring solution. For mission-critical monitoring (a competitor's product launch, regulatory changes that affect your business), don't rely solely on ChatGPT — use dedicated monitoring tools as your primary system and ChatGPT as a supplement.

Third-Party Integrations

ChatGPT can connect to external automation platforms to extend its capabilities:

Zapier: Connect ChatGPT to thousands of apps. Create workflows like: "When I get an email from a specific sender, summarize it and send the summary to Slack."

Make: Similar to Zapier, with more complex workflow capabilities.

Apple Shortcuts (iOS/Mac): Trigger ChatGPT from Shortcuts workflows, or include ChatGPT actions within larger automation sequences. For example, you could create a Shortcut that sends your daily calendar to ChatGPT and returns a prioritized task list.

These integrations turn ChatGPT from a standalone tool into a node in your broader productivity system. Setup specifics change frequently, so check the current documentation for each platform. The key principle: ChatGPT doesn't need to be the center of your workflow — it can be one piece of a larger automation chain, triggered by events in other tools.

Practical integration examples:

Zapier + ChatGPT: "When a new lead fills out our contact form (from Typeform), send their information to ChatGPT to draft a personalized follow-up email, then send that email through Gmail." This turns a 5-minute manual task into a fully automated workflow that responds to leads in seconds.

Apple Shortcuts + ChatGPT: "When I trigger the shortcut, pull my calendar events for tomorrow, send them to ChatGPT, and have it create a prioritized schedule with time blocks for focused work." This turns morning planning into a one-tap automation.

Make + ChatGPT: "When a customer submits a support ticket in Zendesk, send the ticket text to ChatGPT for initial classification (billing, technical, feature request) and draft a first-response template. Route the ticket to the right team with the draft attached." This doesn't replace human support agents — it gives them a head start on every ticket.

Who should use integrations vs. who should skip them: If you're comfortable with automation platforms and you do the same task repeatedly, integrations save real time. If Zapier and Make are unfamiliar territory and your tasks are varied and unpredictable, you'll get more value from ChatGPT's built-in tasks and manual workflows. Don't add integration complexity until the time savings justify it.

When Tasks Are Useful

Tasks work best for: - **Recurring information needs** — Regular research, monitoring, or data gathering - **Reminders** — Personal or professional to-dos with specific timing - **Monitoring** — Watching for changes in prices, news, or status updates - **Routine workflows** — Repetitive tasks that follow the same pattern

Tasks are less useful when: - The task requires real-time judgment or complex decisions - The context changes frequently and requires human interpretation - The task involves sensitive actions (financial transactions, communications to important stakeholders)

Setting Up a Task: Step by Step

Creating a task is conversational. Here's what it looks like in practice:

You: *"Every Sunday evening at 6 PM, search the web for the top 5 news stories about artificial intelligence from the past week and send me a brief summary of each."*

ChatGPT: Confirms the schedule, summarizes what it will do, and asks if you'd like to proceed.

You: Approve, and the task runs automatically every Sunday at 6 PM.

The next Sunday, you'll receive a notification with the summary. If the results aren't what you expected, you can refine: *"Focus more on business applications of AI, less on research papers."*

Practical Task Ideas

Personal: - Morning briefing: weather, calendar summary, and top news at 7 AM - Weekly grocery reminder with a suggested meal plan based on what's in season - Monthly reminder to review subscriptions and cancel unused ones - Flight price monitoring for an upcoming trip

Professional: - Weekly competitor news roundup every Monday morning - Daily summary of industry headlines relevant to your role - Reminder to send weekly status updates every Friday at 2 PM - Monitor a specific regulatory website for new filings

Financial: - Track a stock or cryptocurrency price and alert on significant movements - Monthly reminder to review and categorize expenses - Monitor interest rates if you're planning a major purchase

Health and wellness: - Daily medication reminder at a specific time - Weekly prompt to log your exercise and meals - Monthly reminder to schedule preventive health appointments

Learning: - Daily vocabulary word in a language you're studying - Weekly summary of developments in a topic you're learning about - Periodic quiz on material you're studying for a certification

Managing Your Tasks

You can view, edit, pause, and delete your scheduled tasks through ChatGPT's interface. If a task isn't working as expected, modify it through conversation: *"Change my morning weather update to 6:30 AM instead of 7 AM"* or *"Stop the weekly news summary — I don't need it anymore."*

A practical approach to task management: Don't set up ten tasks at once. Start with one or two that address your most regular needs. Run them for two weeks. If they're consistently useful, add more. If results are inconsistent or off-target, refine the instructions before adding complexity. Many people set up a dozen tasks in an enthusiastic first session, then disable most of them a week later when notifications pile up or the results aren't quite right.

Refining task output: The first run of a scheduled task rarely produces exactly what you want. After your first automated summary, refine: *"The news summary you sent was too detailed. Keep it to three bullet points max, each one sentence. Focus on business and technology news, skip sports and entertainment."* Each refinement improves future runs. Treat the first few executions as calibration rounds.

Limitations to Know

Tasks are still a developing feature. Current limitations include:

- **Notification delivery** depends on having the ChatGPT app installed (mobile) or being logged into the web interface
- **Complex multi-step tasks** may not execute as reliably as simple ones
- **Third-party actions** (actually sending an email, posting to social media) require integrations and explicit permissions
- **Task frequency** has limits depending on your plan tier

- **Location-dependent tasks** (weather, local news) require you to have told ChatGPT your location — either through memories or in the task setup
- **Results can vary** — the same weekly news summary may be excellent one week and mediocre the next, depending on what sources ChatGPT finds

Walkthrough: Building a Personal Morning Briefing

Here's how to set up a daily briefing that actually saves you time:

Step 1: *"Create a daily task that runs at 7 AM every weekday. I want a morning briefing that includes: (1) today's weather for Austin, TX, (2) the top three business news headlines, and (3) any reminders I should know about. Keep the whole thing under 200 words."*

Step 2: After receiving the first briefing, refine it: *"Add a motivational quote at the end. And for the news, focus on tech industry news specifically, not general business."*

Step 3: After a week, evaluate: Is the briefing consistently useful? Are the news items relevant? Is the weather accurate? Adjust based on what you learn.

The goal isn't to automate your whole morning — it's to put the most important information in front of you before you open your inbox. A well-tuned briefing means you start each day with context instead of scrambling to catch up.

Automation is one of the fastest-evolving areas of ChatGPT. What's possible today is a fraction of what will be possible in the coming months. Start with a simple task — a daily weather check or weekly news summary — and build from there as your confidence grows.

In the next chapter, we'll look at Projects — ChatGPT's system for organizing conversations and maintaining context across sessions.

Chapter 19: Projects and Organization

As you use ChatGPT more, your conversation history grows. Finding last week's conversation — let alone last month's — gets harder. Projects solve this by organizing your work into logical groups with persistent context.

What Projects Are

A Project is a folder for related conversations. But it's more than organization — each Project can have:

- **Project Instructions** specific to that project (separate from your global Custom Instructions)
- **Uploaded files** available across every conversation in the project
- **Multiple conversations** that share context

You can set up a Project with specific instructions and reference materials, and every new conversation within it starts with that context already loaded.

Why this matters more than it sounds: Without Projects, the tenth time you start a conversation about your marketing campaign, you're re-explaining your company, your product, your audience, and your campaign goals. With a Project, ChatGPT already knows all of this. Your first message can be *"Draft the email for segment B"* instead of *"I'm working on a marketing campaign for a B2B SaaS product. Our target audience is IT managers at mid-size companies. The campaign budget is $50K. I need to draft an email for segment B, which is..."* The savings compound with every conversation.

Creating a Project

To create a Project:

1. Look for the Projects section in the sidebar
2. Click "New Project"
3. Give it a name and description
4. Add any Project Instructions or files

Practical Examples

Work project: - Name: "Q2 Marketing Campaign" - Project instructions: "I'm leading a marketing campaign for a B2B SaaS product. Our target audience is IT managers at mid-size companies. Our budget is $50K. Always consider our brand voice guidelines." - Uploaded files: Brand guidelines PDF, campaign brief, competitive analysis - Conversations within: brainstorming, content drafts, email copy, reporting analysis

Academic work: - Name: "Thesis Research" - Project instructions: "I'm writing a master's thesis on renewable energy policy. Respond with academic rigor. Always cite sources. Use APA format." - Uploaded files: Literature review, data sets, advisor feedback - Conversations within: Chapter drafts, literature searches, data analysis, methodology discussion

Client work: - Name: "Client: Acme Corp" - Project instructions: "Acme Corp is a retail company with 200 stores. They're modernizing their inventory system. When discussing solutions, consider their existing Oracle infrastructure." - Uploaded files: System architecture docs, project scope, meeting notes - Conversations within: Technical discussions, proposal drafts, status update prep

Personal: - Name: "Home Renovation" - Project instructions: "I'm renovating a 1960s ranch house in Austin, TX. Budget is $80K for kitchen and two bathrooms. I prefer modern-farmhouse style." - Uploaded files: Floor plans, inspiration photos, contractor quotes - Conversations within: Design ideas, material comparisons, budget tracking, contractor communication drafts

Side business: - Name: "Etsy Shop — Candle Co" - Project instructions: "I run a small Etsy shop selling handmade soy candles. My target customer is women aged 25–40 who appreciate artisanal, eco-friendly products. I compete on scent quality and packaging design, not price." - Uploaded files: Product catalog, pricing spreadsheet, brand guidelines, competitor research - Conversations within: New product ideas, listing descriptions, seasonal marketing plans, customer email drafts, inventory planning

Why Projects Matter

Without Projects, every new conversation starts from zero. You re-explain who you are, what you're working on, what constraints apply, and what you've already discussed. Projects eliminate that repetition.

The difference is dramatic. A conversation inside a well-configured Project has the context it needs from the first message — ChatGPT knows the background, has access to reference materials, and follows your project-specific instructions.

Organizing Your Projects

A few organizational principles:

Create Projects for ongoing work, not one-off tasks. A single email draft doesn't need a Project. A multi-week campaign with many conversations does. Rule of thumb: if you'll have more than three conversations about the same topic over more than a week, it deserves a Project.

Keep Project Instructions focused. Don't dump everything you know into a Project's instructions. Include only the context that matters for every conversation within it.

Update files as the project evolves. Swap out stale documents for current ones. Remove files you no longer reference.

Archive completed Projects. When a project wraps up, archive it rather than delete it. The conversations and context stay available if you need them later.

The "active projects" principle: Most people find 3–5 active Projects at any time is the sweet spot. More than that and you spend time deciding which Project a conversation belongs to. Fewer and you're not getting enough organizational value. If you have ten active Projects, some are probably complete and should be archived, or some are too narrow and could be merged.

A tip for writing good Project instructions: Think about what you'd tell a new colleague on their first day working on this project. What would they need to be useful immediately? Company background, project goals, constraints, key stakeholders, terminology specific to this work. That's what goes in Project instructions. Information that changes frequently belongs in uploaded files you can swap out as the project evolves.

Using files effectively: Upload documents ChatGPT needs to reference across multiple conversations: brand guidelines, project briefs, technical specifications, competitive analysis, data sets. Don't upload everything — be selective. A Project with three well-chosen reference documents is more useful than one with thirty files, because ChatGPT can focus on the most relevant material rather than sifting through noise.

Projects vs. Custom Instructions vs. Memory

These three features work together but serve different purposes:

Feature	Scope	Purpose
Memory	All conversations	Persistent facts ChatGPT learns about you
Custom Instructions	All conversations (global)	Your default preferences and context
Project Instructions	Conversations within a Project	Context specific to a project or domain

Think of it as layers: Memory is what ChatGPT knows about you as a person. Custom Instructions are your general preferences. Project Instructions are the specific context for a particular area of work.

How these layers interact in practice: Imagine you have Memory storing "works at a B2B SaaS company," Custom Instructions saying "be concise, use bullet points," and a Project called "Blog Content" with instructions saying "write in a conversational, long-form style." Inside the Blog Content Project, ChatGPT knows you work at a B2B SaaS company (Memory), but it writes in long-form conversational style (Project Instructions) rather than using bullet points (Custom Instructions), because Project Instructions override Custom Instructions in that context. Outside the Project, your bullet-point preference applies again. The layering means you don't have to choose between everyday preferences and project-specific needs — both coexist.

When to use Projects vs. just starting a new conversation: If you'll have more than three conversations about the same topic, create a Project. If it's a one-time question, just start a regular conversation. The threshold is how much context you'd have to re-explain. If you keep pasting the same background into multiple conversations, that's a signal to create a Project and put that background in the Project instructions instead.

Walkthrough: Setting Up a Work Project

Step 1: Create a new Project called "Website Redesign."

Step 2: Add custom instructions: *"I'm leading a website redesign for a mid-size e-commerce company. Our current site runs on Shopify. The target launch is June 2026. The budget is $30K. When discussing design, assume our brand guidelines (uploaded). When discussing tech, assume Shopify Plus capabilities."*

Step 3: Upload reference files: brand guidelines PDF, current site analytics report, competitor screenshots, and the project brief.

Step 4: Start your first conversation within the Project: *"Based on the analytics report and our brand guidelines, what should our homepage redesign priorities be?"*

ChatGPT now has the full context — budget, timeline, platform, brand, and data — without you explaining any of it. Every subsequent conversation in this Project starts from the same foundation. Open a new chat to discuss the checkout flow and you don't need to re-explain the project. The context is already there.

Step 5: As the project evolves, update the files. Replace the old analytics report with the new one. Add the wireframes when they're ready. Remove documents that are no longer relevant.

Tips for Power Users

Name conversations clearly. ChatGPT auto-names conversations, but the names aren't always descriptive enough for a busy Project with many threads. Rename your conversations to something specific: "Homepage wireframe feedback" is more findable than "Chat about design." You can rename by clicking the conversation title in the sidebar.

Use Projects for recurring personal goals too. Projects aren't just for work. Consider setting up Projects for: - **Job search** — upload your resume, target job descriptions, and interview notes - **Health and fitness** — upload your workout plan and dietary goals, track progress in conversations - **Writing a book** — upload your outline, completed chapters, and style notes - **Learning a new skill** — upload learning materials, track your study progress

Combine Projects with GPTs. For maximum leverage, create a Custom GPT for your most common project task, then use it inside the Project. A "Weekly Report Writer" GPT used within your "Q2 Marketing Campaign" Project inherits the Project context while applying the GPT's specialized instructions. The layering produces highly tailored output.

The honest take on Projects: Projects are one of ChatGPT's most underused features — and one of the most valuable for anyone who uses it regularly. Setup is minimal (five minutes for a basic Project), and the savings per conversation are real (you skip the context-setting step every time). If you use ChatGPT daily and you're not using Projects, you're doing more work than you need to.

Projects separate casual ChatGPT users from people who get serious value out of it daily. In the next chapter, we'll look at Custom GPTs — another way to build specialized, purpose-built AI experiences.

Chapter 20: GPTs and the GPT Store

Custom GPTs are specialized versions of ChatGPT built for specific tasks. Think of them as apps within ChatGPT — each one has its own instructions, knowledge base, and personality, optimized for a particular use case.

What Custom GPTs Are

A Custom GPT is a configured version of ChatGPT with:

- **Custom Instructions** that define its behavior, expertise, and personality
- **Uploaded knowledge files** it can reference (documents, data, guides)
- **Specific tools enabled** (web browsing, DALL-E, Code Interpreter)
- **A name, description, and icon** that help users find and understand it

Anyone on a Plus, Pro, or Business plan can create Custom GPTs — no coding required.

Using GPTs from the Store

The GPT Store is a directory of Custom GPTs created by OpenAI and the community. To browse it:

1. Click "Explore GPTs" in the sidebar
2. Browse by category or search for a specific need
3. Click a GPT to start using it

Popular categories include:

- **Writing** — Blog post generators, email assistants, copywriting tools
- **Productivity** — Meeting summarizers, project planners, scheduling helpers
- **Education** — Math tutors, language teachers, study aids
- **Programming** — Code reviewers, debugging assistants, documentation generators

- **Creative** – Story writers, image prompt crafters, game designers
- **Research** – Academic assistants, data analysts, market researchers
- **Lifestyle** – Fitness coaches, recipe generators, travel planners

The quality of community GPTs varies widely. Check the ratings and number of users, and try a few conversations before relying on one for important work.

How to evaluate a GPT before committing: Test it with a request where you already know what the answer should be. If it's a writing GPT, give it a task you've done before and compare the output to what you'd produce yourself. If it's a research GPT, ask it something you already know and check for accuracy. Many community GPTs are built by enthusiasts who are good at prompting but haven't tested their GPT against edge cases. A few test messages will tell you whether it's useful or just a thin wrapper around generic ChatGPT.

The honest take on the GPT Store: The Store has some useful GPTs – especially the ones built by companies for their own products (like Canva's design GPT or Consensus for academic research). But most community GPTs are mediocre. They're often just a system prompt you could write yourself in Custom Instructions. Before searching the Store, ask: could I just tell ChatGPT to do this in a regular conversation? If yes, you probably don't need a Custom GPT for it.

Creating Your Own GPT

Creating a GPT is a conversation:

1. Click "Create a GPT" in the sidebar
2. ChatGPT guides you through the setup process, asking what you want the GPT to do
3. You describe the purpose, behavior, and personality
4. Upload any files you want it to reference
5. Configure which tools it should have access to
6. Name it, add a description, and choose an icon
7. Choose whether it's private (just you), shared (via link), or public (in the GPT Store)

Example: You could create a GPT called "Company Style Guide Checker" that has your company's style guide uploaded, with instructions to review any text you paste in and flag deviations from the guide. Every time you need to check content, you open that GPT instead of generic ChatGPT.

A step-by-step walkthrough of creating your first GPT:

Say you want a GPT that helps you write LinkedIn posts in your style.

1. Click "Create a GPT" in the sidebar
2. ChatGPT asks what you want to build. Say: *"A LinkedIn post writer that matches my writing style. I'll upload examples of my past posts."*
3. ChatGPT suggests a name, description, and initial instructions. Review and refine.
4. Upload 5–10 of your best LinkedIn posts as a reference file. Tell the GPT: *"Always match the tone, structure, and style of these example posts."*
5. In the instructions, add specifics: *"My posts are always between 100-200 words. I use short paragraphs (1-2 sentences each). I never use hashtags. I always end with a question to drive engagement. I write about leadership and product management."*
6. Test: ask for a post about a recent topic and see if it sounds like you.
7. Refine the instructions based on what's off.
8. Set it to "Only me" (private) since it's for personal use.

The whole process takes about 15 minutes. The result is a tool you can pull up every time you need to write a LinkedIn post — give it the topic and it produces a draft that already sounds like you.

Actions: Connecting GPTs to External Services

For more advanced GPTs, you can configure *Actions* — the ability for your GPT to call external APIs (application programming interfaces). This means your GPT can:

- Look up real-time data from your company's systems
- Submit information to external services
- Pull in data from third-party APIs (weather, stock prices, CRM records)
- Trigger workflows in other tools

Setting up Actions requires technical knowledge — you define the API endpoints and authentication. The result is a GPT that doesn't just reference uploaded documents; it connects to live systems.

Example: A "Sales Dashboard" GPT with an Action connected to your CRM API. Ask *"How many deals did we close this week?"* and it queries your CRM in real time instead of relying on an uploaded spreadsheet that may be stale.

Actions are an advanced feature, and most users will never need them. But if you have development resources, they turn a GPT from a smart document reader into an integrated business tool.

GPT Ideas

Here are GPTs that people commonly build:

For work: - Onboarding buddy — Answers new employee questions using the employee handbook - RFP responder — Drafts responses using your company's past proposals and capabilities - Customer email assistant — Follows your company's tone and knows your products

For personal use: - Meal planner — Knows your dietary restrictions and preferences - Workout coach — Designed for your fitness level and equipment availability - Travel planner — Knows your travel preferences, budget, and past trips

For teams: - Meeting note formatter — Takes messy notes and formats them to your team's standard template - Code reviewer — Reviews code against your team's coding standards - Content brief generator — Creates briefs following your content team's template

Sharing GPTs

Once you've created a GPT, you can:

- **Keep it private** — Only you can use it
- **Share via link** — Anyone with the link can use it (great for teams)
- **Publish to the GPT Store** — Available to all ChatGPT users

If you publish to the store, other users can find and use your GPT. OpenAI has a review process for published GPTs to ensure quality and safety.

Tips for Building Effective GPTs

Be specific in your instructions. Vague instructions produce vague GPTs. Instead of "Help with marketing," try "You are a social media content strategist specializing in LinkedIn posts for B2B SaaS companies. Generate post ideas, draft copy, and suggest engagement strategies."

Upload relevant files. The more context your GPT has, the more useful it is. Style guides, templates, FAQs, product documentation — anything that helps it do its job.

Test thoroughly. Try your GPT with various prompts, including edge cases. Refine the instructions based on where it falls short.

Keep it focused. A GPT that tries to do everything will do nothing well. Build separate GPTs for separate tasks.

Iterate. Your first version won't be perfect. Use it for a while, note what works and what doesn't, and update the instructions.

A common pitfall: Many people create GPTs with long, complex instructions that try to anticipate every scenario. This usually backfires — the GPT gets confused by contradictory instructions or overrides itself. Start with 3–5 clear instructions and add more only when you hit a specific situation the GPT handles poorly. The best GPTs have focused instructions, not comprehensive ones.

GPTs vs. Projects vs. Custom Instructions

These three features overlap, so it's worth clarifying when to use each:

Feature	Best For	Persistence
Custom Instructions	Your personal defaults across all conversations	Always active
Projects	Organizing ongoing work with shared files and context	Active within the Project

Feature	Best For	Persistence
Custom GPTs	A reusable, shareable tool for a specific task	Standalone — can be shared with others

Rule of thumb: If only you will use it, a Project is simpler. If you want to share it with your team or the public, build a GPT. If it should apply to every conversation you have, use Custom Instructions.

When to Build a GPT vs. Just Use a Good Prompt

This is the question most people struggle with. Here's a clear framework:

Build a GPT when: - You do the same type of task regularly (weekly or more) - The task requires uploaded reference files (style guides, templates, data) - You want to share the capability with others - The instructions are complex enough that re-typing them each time is impractical

Just use a prompt when: - The task is one-off or occasional - No reference files are needed - The instructions are simple enough to type in a message - You don't need to share the capability

Many things people build GPTs for could be handled equally well with a good prompt saved in a text file you paste at the start of a conversation. The overhead of creating, maintaining, and navigating to a GPT only pays off when you use it frequently or need to share it. For everything else, a well-crafted prompt is simpler and more flexible.

Custom GPTs let you build purpose-built AI tools without writing a line of code. In the next chapter, we'll look at how ChatGPT connects to external services and data sources.

Chapter 21: Connectors and Integrations

ChatGPT doesn't have to work in isolation. Through connectors and integrations, it can access your files, read your email, pull data from business tools, and fit into the workflows you already use.

MCP Access Connectors

MCP (Model Context Protocol) is an open standard — originally developed by Anthropic — that allows AI assistants to connect directly to external services. OpenAI adopted MCP for ChatGPT's connector system. These connectors are primarily available on Business and Enterprise plans, though some are accessible on individual plans.

Current connectors include services like:

- **Google Drive** — Access and analyze documents, spreadsheets, and presentations stored in your Drive
- **OneDrive** — Microsoft's cloud storage integration for Office 365 users
- **Gmail** — Read (not send) emails for reference and context when preparing responses or summaries
- **Amplitude** — Product analytics data for teams tracking user behavior
- **Stripe** — Payment and subscription data for revenue analysis
- **Monday.com** — Project management data for tracking tasks and timelines
- **Semrush** — SEO and marketing data for content strategy
- **And more** — The connector ecosystem is growing regularly, with new services added quarterly

Which connectors matter most? For most individuals, Google Drive and Gmail (or OneDrive for Microsoft users) are the highest-value connectors — they give ChatGPT access to your most-used documents and communications. For business teams, the value depends on your tech stack: if your company lives in

Salesforce, a Salesforce connector changes everything; if you don't use Salesforce, it's irrelevant. Evaluate connectors by how often you currently download data from a service just to feed it to ChatGPT. If you do it daily, that connector is worth enabling.

How Connectors Work

When you enable a connector, ChatGPT can read data from that service within your conversations. For example:

"Look at the latest version of the Q2 report in my Google Drive and summarize the financial highlights."

"Check my Gmail for emails from [client name] this week and summarize any action items."

"Pull our website traffic data from the last 30 days and tell me which pages are performing best."

Important: Most connectors are read-only. ChatGPT can access and analyze data from these services, but it typically can't modify data, send messages, or take actions within them. This is a deliberate safety measure.

Why read-only matters: Read-only means you can ask ChatGPT to analyze your Gmail without worrying it will accidentally send an email, or pull data from your Google Drive without fear it will edit a shared document. Connectors are safe to try — worst case, ChatGPT reads something you didn't intend, not takes an action you didn't want. Write capabilities may be added for some services as connectors evolve, but they'll always require explicit permission before taking action.

Practical connector prompts:

"Check my Google Drive for any documents modified in the last week related to the Henderson project. Summarize what changed."

"Look at my recent Gmail messages from anyone at Acme Corp. Are there any action items I haven't addressed?"

"Pull the last 30 days of traffic data from our analytics connector. What pages are trending up? What's declining?"

Connectors eliminate the manual step of downloading data, uploading it to ChatGPT, and providing context. With a connected Google Drive, "look at the Q2 report" is enough — ChatGPT finds it, reads it, and works with it directly.

Setting Up Connectors

The setup process varies by connector but generally involves:

1. Go to Settings → Connectors (or look for the connector option in your workspace)
2. Select the service you want to connect
3. Authenticate with that service (you'll be redirected to log in)
4. Grant the specific permissions ChatGPT needs
5. Start using it in your conversations

Authentication is typically OAuth-based — you're redirected to the service's own login page (Google, Microsoft, etc.) and grant specific permissions. ChatGPT never sees or stores your password. You can revoke access at any time by going back to the connector settings or by revoking permissions from the connected service's own security settings.

A tip for first-time setup: Before connecting a service, think about what data the connector will have access to. A Google Drive connector grants ChatGPT access to every file in your Drive — not just the ones you mention. ChatGPT only reads files you specifically reference, but the breadth of access is worth understanding. If your Drive contains sensitive documents you'd rather keep separate, consider using a dedicated Google account for ChatGPT-connected work.

Admins on Business and Enterprise plans can manage which connectors are available to their teams.

Working with Cloud Files

Even without formal connectors, you can work with cloud files by uploading them directly:

- Download a file from Google Drive or OneDrive
- Upload it to ChatGPT

- Work with it in your conversation

This manual approach works on any plan. Connectors simply make the process seamless by eliminating the download/upload step.

The honest take on connectors vs. manual upload: For most individuals and small teams, the manual download-upload approach works fine. Connectors save maybe 30 seconds per interaction — meaningful at ten times a day, negligible at once a week. Connectors become valuable for teams on Business or Enterprise plans working with shared documents constantly. When five people on a team can all say "look at the Q2 report in Drive" without anyone downloading and uploading anything, the friction reduction compounds.

Walkthrough: Using Google Drive Connector

Once connected, working with Drive files feels natural:

You: *"Find the 'Project Roadmap Q2' spreadsheet in my Google Drive."*

ChatGPT: Locates the file and confirms the title, last modified date, and owner.

You: *"Summarize the key milestones and flag any that are past due."*

ChatGPT: Reads the spreadsheet, identifies milestones, and highlights overdue items — all without you downloading, uploading, or leaving the conversation.

You: *"Draft a status update email based on this data. Highlight the overdue items diplomatically."*

The connector eliminates the friction of downloading a file, uploading it to ChatGPT, and managing file versions. Small change in workflow, significant gain in speed — especially for teams that reference shared documents constantly.

ChatGPT in Your Existing Workflow

Beyond formal connectors, there are several ways to integrate ChatGPT into your daily work:

Browser extension/app: Keep ChatGPT open alongside your work. On desktop, a keyboard shortcut brings it up instantly.

Copy-paste workflow: Copy text from any application, paste it into ChatGPT for analysis or improvement, then paste the result back. Simple but effective.

API access: For more technical users, OpenAI's API lets you build ChatGPT into custom applications and workflows. This is beyond the scope of this book but worth knowing about if you have development resources.

Microsoft Copilot: If your organization uses Microsoft 365, Microsoft Copilot (powered by OpenAI's technology) brings AI assistance directly into Word, Excel, PowerPoint, and Outlook. Different product from ChatGPT, related technology underneath. Some organizations use both — Copilot for in-app assistance within Office documents, ChatGPT for broader research, analysis, and creative work.

Bookmarklets and browser shortcuts: Some users create simple browser bookmarks that open ChatGPT with pre-filled context from the current page. A lightweight alternative to Atlas for users who aren't ready to switch browsers.

The ChatGPT + Slack workflow: Many teams don't need formal connectors — they need a workflow. A common pattern: someone asks a question in a Slack channel. Another team member copies the question, pastes it into ChatGPT (with relevant context), gets an answer, and pastes the response back. This "human in the loop" pattern works for teams that aren't ready for formal automation but want to share AI output across the group.

Finding your integration sweet spot: The most common mistake is trying to connect everything. Start with one integration that addresses your biggest pain point. If you're constantly downloading files from Google Drive to analyze in ChatGPT, connect Google Drive. If you spend a lot of time pulling up client emails before meetings, connect Gmail. Add more connections only when the first is saving you meaningful time. Over-connected systems create complexity (and security considerations) without proportional benefit.

Privacy and Connector Security

When connecting external services:

- Review the permissions each connector requests
- Understand that data flowing through connectors is processed by OpenAI
- On Business and Enterprise plans, data from connectors is not used for model training

- On individual plans, check your data controls settings
- Regularly review your connected services and revoke access for any you no longer need
- Be especially cautious with connectors that access sensitive data (email, financial information)

Walkthrough: Using Connectors for Meeting Prep

Here's a practical workflow that demonstrates why connectors matter:

Without connectors: Before a client meeting, you download the project brief from Google Drive, upload it to ChatGPT, download the latest emails from Gmail, copy-paste relevant messages into ChatGPT, and then ask for help preparing talking points. Setup time: 5–10 minutes.

With connectors: *"I have a meeting with the Acme Corp team in an hour. Check my Google Drive for the latest Acme project documents. Also check my Gmail for recent messages from anyone at acme.com. Based on what you find, prepare talking points for the meeting and flag any unresolved issues."* Setup time: 30 seconds.

Connectors eliminate the manual data-gathering step. For one meeting, savings are modest. For someone with five meetings a day, they compound to an hour or more per week.

The Future of Integrations

The connector ecosystem is one of ChatGPT's fastest-evolving areas. New integrations land regularly, and existing connectors gain capabilities over time. OpenAI has signaled that connectors will eventually support write operations (sending emails, updating CRM records, modifying documents) — not just reading data. When that lands, ChatGPT moves from research-and-analysis assistant to execution assistant, taking action on your behalf within connected services.

For now, check ChatGPT's settings periodically to see what's new. If you're evaluating Business or Enterprise plans for your organization, the available connectors belong in your evaluation criteria — they determine how deeply ChatGPT can integrate with your existing workflows.

In the next chapter, we'll look at Memory and Personalization — how ChatGPT learns about you and adapts to your preferences over time.

Chapter 22: Memory and Personalization

The more ChatGPT knows about you, the more useful it becomes. Memory and personalization features let ChatGPT learn from your conversations and adapt to your preferences over time.

How Memory Works

Memory is ChatGPT's ability to retain information across conversations. When you mention something important — your name, your job, a preference, an ongoing project — ChatGPT can store it as a memory and reference it later.

If you mention in one conversation that you're a vegetarian, ChatGPT will remember when you ask for recipe suggestions later. Tell it you prefer concise responses, and it adjusts going forward.

Memory happens in two ways:

Automatic: ChatGPT picks up on relevant information as you chat and stores it without being asked. It's selective — it doesn't memorize every detail, just things it judges to be useful for future conversations.

Explicit: You can tell ChatGPT to remember something: *"Remember that my team uses Jira for project management"* or *"Remember that I prefer bullet points over paragraphs."*

What kinds of things does ChatGPT remember? Typically: your name, your job and industry, your location, your preferences (communication style, formatting, level of detail), ongoing projects, dietary restrictions, family details you've shared, technical tools you use, and learning goals. It won't remember the specifics of a conversation from last Tuesday — it stores distilled facts, not transcripts.

An important nuance: ChatGPT's automatic memory isn't perfect at deciding what's worth remembering. It might store something trivial ("user mentioned they had pizza for dinner") while missing something important ("user is transitioning to a new role in three weeks"). That's why explicit memory management matters. If something is important to you, tell ChatGPT to remember it explicitly rather than hoping it picks up on it.

Managing Your Memories

You have full control over what ChatGPT remembers:

View memories: Go to Settings → Personalization → Memory. You'll see a list of everything ChatGPT has stored.

Delete individual memories: Remove any specific memory you don't want retained.

Clear all memories: Wipe everything and start fresh.

Turn off memory entirely: If you don't want ChatGPT to remember anything across conversations, toggle Memory off in settings.

Review regularly. Memories can become outdated. If you changed jobs, moved cities, or shifted preferences, check that ChatGPT's memories reflect your current situation.

How to do a memory audit: Go to Settings, then Personalization, then Memory. Read through every stored memory. You'll find a mix: useful facts ("works as a product manager at a fintech startup"), outdated information ("is preparing for a job interview" from three months ago), and oddly specific items you don't need ("mentioned they like Thai food"). Delete anything stale or unnecessary, and add anything important that's missing. Doing this monthly keeps memory clean and ensures ChatGPT works from accurate information.

A memory trick that pays off: After a significant life change — new job, new city, new project — tell ChatGPT: *"I want to update my memories. Here's what's changed: [list changes]. Please update your memories to reflect this and delete any memories that are now outdated."* ChatGPT walks through its stored memories with you and updates them. Faster than going through the settings interface item by item.

Custom Instructions (Advanced)

We introduced Custom Instructions in Chapter 3. Here's how to use them at a more advanced level.

The "About You" field works best with structured, specific information:

> I'm a product manager at a Series B fintech startup (150 employees). I manage a team of 3. I report to the VP of Product. Our product is a B2B payment processing platform. Our customers are mid-size e-commerce companies. I'm technical enough to read code but I don't write it. I have an MBA and 8 years of product experience.

This gives ChatGPT a rich understanding of your perspective, which shapes every response.

The "Response Preferences" field is where you control ChatGPT's behavior:

> Be direct and concise. Lead with the answer, then explain if needed. Use bullet points for lists. Don't use corporate jargon or buzzwords. If I ask for a recommendation, commit to one — don't give me five options with "it depends." Challenge my assumptions when you think I'm wrong. Format code blocks properly.

These instructions apply to every conversation unless overridden by Project-specific instructions.

The interaction between Custom Instructions and Project Instructions: Custom Instructions are your defaults. Project Instructions override them inside that Project. The layering is powerful. Your Custom Instructions might say "be concise and use bullet points," while your "Blog Writing" Project says "use flowing prose, not bullet points." Inside the Project, Project Instructions win. Outside any Project, Custom Instructions apply. It's the difference between your everyday personality and how you act in specific professional contexts — same person, different mode.

Common Custom Instructions that make a big difference: - *"Never start a response with 'Great question!' or 'Absolutely!' or 'Certainly!' — just answer."* (Removes annoying preamble) - *"When I ask for a recommendation, commit to one option and explain why. Don't give me five options with 'it depends.'"*

(Forces decisiveness) - *"If I'm wrong about something, correct me directly. Don't agree with incorrect statements."* (Reduces sycophancy) - *"Default to metric units"* or *"Default to imperial units"* (Matches your preferences) - *"I'm in [timezone]. When I ask about time-sensitive things, use my local time."* (Prevents confusion)

Temporary Chat

Temporary Chat (introduced in Chapter 3) is the counterpart to Memory — a per-conversation mode where no memories are created or accessed, and the conversation doesn't appear in your history. Use it when you want a clean, private interaction. The key point for personalization: Temporary Chat lets you step outside your personalized ChatGPT when you need to.

When to reach for Temporary Chat:

- Your memories or Custom Instructions might bias the response in a direction you don't want
- You're testing prompts and don't want to pollute your history
- You want a "clean" ChatGPT experience without your personalization

Shaping ChatGPT Over Time

Memory, Custom Instructions, and regular use combine to create a ChatGPT that's increasingly tailored to you. After a few weeks of active use, you'll notice:

- It references your preferences without being reminded
- Its tone matches what you prefer
- It considers your context when making suggestions
- It builds on previous conversations naturally

This is one of ChatGPT's strongest advantages over stateless AI interfaces. Personalization compounds, making each interaction more efficient and relevant.

Tips for Effective Personalization

Be explicit about preferences early. Don't wait for ChatGPT to infer your preferences from dozens of conversations. Tell it upfront: *"I prefer detailed technical responses"* or *"Keep things high-level unless I ask for details."*

Correct misunderstandings. If ChatGPT applies a memory incorrectly, correct it: *"I no longer work at that company"* or *"I've changed my mind about preferring bullet points — use prose."*

Use Projects for context switching. If you use ChatGPT for very different purposes (technical work vs. personal tasks), use Projects to maintain separate contexts rather than trying to make a single set of Custom Instructions work for everything.

Don't fight the personalization. Some people reset their memories frequently or avoid Custom Instructions because they want "neutral" ChatGPT. A personalized ChatGPT is meaningfully more useful. Embrace it.

Think of it like training a new assistant. The first week, you explain everything — who you are, what you do, how you like things done. By the end of the month, the assistant anticipates your needs. ChatGPT's personalization works the same way. The investment in Custom Instructions and explicit memories during your first few weeks pays dividends for months. Every conversation starts faster and produces more relevant output because the foundation is in place.

When personalization works against you: Stored context can bias responses in unhelpful ways. If you're a marketing professional and ChatGPT knows that, it may frame every answer through a marketing lens — even when you're asking about something personal. When you notice this, use Temporary Chat for the off-topic conversation, or explicitly say: *"Set aside everything you know about my work. I'm asking this as a regular person, not a marketer."*

Walkthrough: Building Your Custom Instructions

Here's a practical approach to setting up effective Custom Instructions from scratch:

Day 1: Start with the basics — your name, role, and one or two response preferences.

> About me: I'm Jordan, a marketing manager at a B2B tech company.
> How to respond: Be concise. Use bullet points for lists.

Week 1: After several conversations, you'll notice patterns in what you keep asking for. Add those.

About me: I'm Jordan, a marketing manager at a B2B tech company. My team is 4 people. I report to the CMO. Our product is an enterprise analytics platform. I'm comfortable with data but I'm not technical. How to respond: Be concise. Use bullet points for lists. When I ask for content, match our brand voice: professional but not corporate, confident but not salesy. Don't hedge — commit to recommendations.

Month 1: Refine based on what's working and what isn't.

[Previous content, plus:] Don't start responses with "Great question!" or "Certainly!" Just answer. When I ask for a plan, include timelines and owner suggestions. Default to markdown tables for comparisons.

The best Custom Instructions evolve over time. Treat them as a living document, not a one-time setup.

The Compounding Value of Personalization

After three months of active use, a well-personalized ChatGPT account saves real time on every interaction. You skip the context-setting phase. You skip the "please don't use bullet points" correction phase. You skip the "I'm in the marketing department at a tech company" preamble. Every conversation starts further ahead because the groundwork is laid.

A before-and-after comparison: Without personalization, a typical request might be: *"I'm a product manager at a fintech startup. I need to write a stakeholder update email. We use OKRs. I prefer concise communication with clear action items. The tone should be professional but not stiff. Draft an update about the Q2 product launch."* With good personalization: *"Draft a stakeholder update about the Q2 product launch."* ChatGPT already knows your role, company, communication style, and formatting preferences. The request drops from 60 words to 10, and the output quality is identical or better because the stored context is more comprehensive and consistent than what you'd include in a manual prompt.

This is why fifteen minutes setting up Custom Instructions and managing your memories is one of the highest-leverage activities you can do with ChatGPT. The investment pays for itself within a few days of regular use.

Next up: Atlas — OpenAI's AI browser that puts ChatGPT alongside you everywhere you go on the web.

Chapter 23: Atlas — The AI Browser

Atlas is a web browser built by OpenAI with ChatGPT at its core. Instead of ChatGPT being a separate tool you switch to, Atlas puts it right next to you as you browse — understanding the pages you visit, answering questions about what you're reading, and completing tasks in context.

What Atlas Is

Atlas is built on Chromium (the same engine behind Google Chrome) and looks and feels like a modern web browser. What makes it different is the ChatGPT sidebar — an AI assistant that's always available and always aware of what you're looking at.

Why this matters: Using ChatGPT in a regular browser tab requires constant context-switching — copy text, switch to ChatGPT tab, paste, read response, switch back. With Atlas, the AI sits beside the page you're reading. You never leave the page. You never copy-paste. You ask, and Atlas already knows what you're looking at. Sounds like a small difference, but after a day with Atlas, going back to tab-switching feels clunky. The friction reduction changes how often you reach for AI — from "when I have a big enough question to justify switching tabs" to "whenever a thought crosses my mind."

Key Features

Sidebar assistant. A ChatGPT panel lives alongside your browser. It can: - Summarize the page you're reading - Answer questions about the content - Rewrite selected text - Translate content - Extract data from what's on screen

Contextual awareness. Unlike using ChatGPT in a separate tab, Atlas knows what you're browsing. You can ask *"What are the key points of this article?"* without copy-pasting anything.

Agent Mode in Atlas. Agent Mode works within Atlas with improvements that make it faster and more contextual. It can research across tabs, automate form filling, and plan events or book appointments while you browse.

Standard browser features. Atlas supports extensions, bookmarks, tabs, and everything you'd expect from a Chromium browser. You can use it as your primary browser.

Current Availability

As of May 2026: - **macOS:** Available to Free, Plus, Pro, and Go users - **Business and Enterprise:** Available in beta (if enabled by admin) - **Windows, iOS, Android:** Coming soon

What "coming soon" means for you: If you're on Windows or mobile, you can't use Atlas yet. The good news: everything Atlas does with its sidebar can be approximated by keeping a ChatGPT tab open alongside your browser — just less seamless. When Windows and mobile versions launch, the transition will be straightforward since your ChatGPT account, conversations, and settings carry over automatically.

For business decision-makers: If your team is on macOS, Atlas is worth piloting now. If your team is mixed Mac and Windows, wait for the Windows version before standardizing on Atlas — you don't want half your team on a different workflow.

The Superapp Vision

OpenAI has announced plans to merge ChatGPT, Codex (their coding platform), and Atlas into a single desktop application. This "superapp" would unify all of OpenAI's tools into one interface rather than separate products.

What this means for you: Atlas is likely the future of how many people will interact with ChatGPT — not as a separate website you visit, but as an integrated layer across everything you do on your computer.

Why the superapp matters beyond convenience: Merging browsing, AI conversation, and coding into a single application reflects a broader trend: AI is moving from a tool you use to an environment you work in. Instead of switching between Chrome for browsing, ChatGPT for AI, and VS Code for coding, you have one unified workspace where all three are always available. For non-technical users, AI assistance becomes as ambient as spell-check — always present, always available, no extra steps to access.

What this means for your workflow now: Even before the superapp ships, you can prepare by integrating ChatGPT more tightly into daily work. Use the desktop app with keyboard shortcuts. Try Atlas if you're on macOS. Build the muscle memory of reaching for AI throughout your day. When these tools merge, you'll be ready.

Using Atlas: Practical Scenarios

Research while reading. You're reading a news article about a new climate policy. Instead of opening ChatGPT in another tab, you ask the sidebar: *"What are the key criticisms of this policy?"* Atlas reads the article and provides context-aware analysis without you copying anything.

Shopping decisions. You're on a product page for a laptop. You ask the sidebar: *"Compare this laptop's specs to the MacBook Air M4. Which is better for video editing?"* Atlas reads the specs from the page and delivers a direct comparison.

Form filling with context. You're filling out a job application. Agent Mode in Atlas can see the form fields, pull information from your resume (if you've provided it), and help you craft responses — all while looking at the actual page.

Summarizing research. You have twelve tabs open on a topic. You ask Atlas to *"Summarize the key points from my open tabs about renewable energy storage."* It works across your browsing context instead of requiring you to feed content in one page at a time.

Language assistance. You're browsing a website in German. Atlas can translate the page and answer questions about the content in English without leaving the page or opening a separate translation tool.

Writing assistance while browsing. You're reading a competitor's marketing page and need to write a comparison for your team. Ask: *"Based on what's on this page, draft a bullet-point comparison between their product and ours. Here are our key features: [list]."* Atlas reads the competitor's page and produces the comparison without you copying or summarizing.

Email drafting from context. You're on a product page for a tool your team is evaluating. Ask: *"Draft an email to my manager recommending we try this tool. Pull the key features and pricing from this page."* Atlas extracts the relevant information and writes the email, all without leaving the page.

The honest take on Atlas: If you use ChatGPT multiple times a day while browsing, Atlas is a real quality-of-life upgrade. If you use ChatGPT a few times a week for standalone tasks (writing, brainstorming, research), the benefit of switching browsers is minimal. Atlas scales with how often you need AI while actively browsing — the more web-integrated your AI usage, the more sense Atlas makes.

Extension Compatibility

Since Atlas is built on Chromium, many Chrome extensions work — password managers, ad blockers, and productivity tools install and run normally. Not every Chrome extension is guaranteed to work, though, and the Atlas extension ecosystem is still maturing. Before switching, check that your must-have extensions function correctly. Common extensions like 1Password, Bitwarden, uBlock Origin, and Grammarly typically work fine. More specialized or niche extensions may not.

Multiple Account Support

Atlas supports multiple ChatGPT accounts, which is useful if you have a personal account and a work account. You can switch between them without logging out and back in.

Privacy in Atlas

When you browse in Atlas, the sidebar can see the content of the pages you visit — that's what makes contextual awareness possible. If you visit a page but don't invoke the sidebar, it's standard browser behavior. Once you ask the sidebar "summarize this page," the page content is sent to OpenAI for processing. Apply the same data hygiene with Atlas as with ChatGPT: don't ask the sidebar to analyze pages with sensitive information (banking, medical records, confidential documents) unless you're on a Business or Enterprise plan with appropriate data protections.

Should You Switch to Atlas?

Switch if: - You frequently use ChatGPT while browsing the web - You often copy-paste content between your browser and ChatGPT - You want Agent Mode to work with the pages you're already on - You use macOS (for now)

Wait if: - You're deeply invested in Chrome extensions that Atlas may not support yet - You're on Windows (it's coming but not yet available) - Your browser workflow is complex and switching would be disruptive

Atlas vs. Using ChatGPT in a Browser Tab

Aspect	Atlas Sidebar	ChatGPT in a Tab
Context awareness	Sees your current page	Requires copy-paste
Switching cost	None — it's right there	Tab switching
Agent Mode	Works with your browsing context	Works independently
Browser compatibility	macOS only (for now)	Any browser, any OS
Extension support	Growing but limited	N/A (it's a website)
Account management	Multiple accounts supported	One account per session

Getting Started with Atlas

If you want to try Atlas, here's a practical approach:

1. Download Atlas from OpenAI's website (macOS only as of May 2026)
2. Log in with your existing ChatGPT account
3. Import your bookmarks from Chrome (Atlas supports standard Chromium bookmark import)
4. Install your essential extensions
5. Use Atlas as a secondary browser for a week — don't commit to switching yet
6. After a week, evaluate: Did the sidebar make a meaningful difference in how you use AI? Did you reach for it more often than you would have switched to a ChatGPT tab?

The trial approach works best because Atlas's value is experiential. Reading about it doesn't capture the difference — you have to feel the friction reduction firsthand. Some people try it and immediately switch. Others decide the browser-switching cost isn't worth it. Both are valid, and you won't know which camp you're in until you try.

A word of caution about switching browsers: Your current browser has years of saved passwords, autofill data, extensions, and muscle memory behind it. Don't switch cold turkey. Run Atlas alongside your current browser for at least two weeks before deciding. And make sure your password manager works in Atlas before you rely on it — browser switching without your password manager is a recipe for frustration.

Atlas represents where AI assistants are heading: not separate tools you switch to, but intelligent layers embedded in the software you already use.

With that, we've covered every major feature in ChatGPT's toolkit. Part V shifts focus from *what* ChatGPT can do to *how* to get the most out of it — starting with the art and science of prompting.

Part VI: Getting Better Results

"It's not that we need better AI. We need to learn to ask better questions."

— Fei-Fei Li

Chapter 24: Prompting Fundamentals

You've been using ChatGPT throughout this book, picking up prompting basics from the examples. This chapter formalizes those instincts into principles that consistently improve your results.

A prompt is what you type into ChatGPT. Prompting is the skill of typing things that produce great responses. No magic formulas, no secret words — just clear communication.

The Five Elements of an Effective Prompt

Most great prompts include some combination of these elements:

1. Role

Tell ChatGPT who to be.

"You are an experienced hiring manager at a Fortune 500 company..." "Act as a patient, encouraging math tutor..." "You are a food critic writing for a local newspaper..."

A role activates relevant knowledge and sets tone. A "sympathetic counselor" responds differently from a "blunt executive coach" to the same question.

2. Task

State clearly what you want done.

"Write a product description..." "Create a weekly meal plan..." "Analyze this data and identify trends..." "Explain how this concept works..."

Be specific about the deliverable. "Help me with my resume" is vague. "Rewrite the experience section of my resume to emphasize leadership" is actionable.

3. Context

Provide the background information needed.

"I'm a small business owner with 10 employees..." "This is for a presentation to non-technical executives..." "The audience is college freshmen who have no background in economics..."

Context shapes everything. The same question produces wildly different answers depending on who's asking and why.

4. Format

Specify how you want the response structured.

"Respond in bullet points..." "Give me a numbered list of steps..." "Format this as a table with three columns..." "Keep it under 200 words..." "Write it as an email..."

If you don't specify a format, ChatGPT picks one. It usually picks reasonably, but you'll get better results being explicit.

5. Constraints

Define boundaries and limitations.

"Don't use technical jargon..." "Only consider options under $500..." "Focus on the last two years of data..." "Don't suggest anything that requires coding..."

Constraints prevent ChatGPT from going in directions you don't want.

Putting It Together

Here's a prompt that uses all five elements:

"You are a senior financial advisor specializing in retirement planning [ROLE]. Create a simple, actionable guide [TASK] for someone in their early 30s who earns $80K/year and has $15K in savings but no retirement accounts [CONTEXT]. Format it as 5 numbered steps, each with a one-paragraph explanation [FORMAT]. Avoid recommending specific stocks or funds — focus on strategy and account types [CONSTRAINTS]."

Not every prompt needs all five elements. A quick factual question needs none. But when response quality matters, adding even one or two elements dramatically improves the output.

Try this experiment: Take a task you use ChatGPT for regularly. Write the prompt with zero elements (just the bare request). Then write it again with all five. Compare. The difference is usually stark. The five-element prompt produces output that feels written for you and your situation. The bare prompt produces something generic that could have been written for anyone.

A real-world example:

Bare prompt: *"Write a LinkedIn post."*

Five-element prompt: *"You are a thought leader in product management [ROLE]. Write a LinkedIn post about why most product roadmaps fail [TASK]. I'm a VP of Product at a Series C startup with 200 employees [CONTEXT]. Format: 150-200 words, short paragraphs, end with a question [FORMAT]. Don't use buzzwords like 'synergy' or 'leverage' — write like a real person [CONSTRAINTS]."*

The bare prompt produces a generic, forgettable LinkedIn post. The five-element prompt produces a post that sounds like a specific person with a specific perspective, targeted at a specific audience. That's the difference between content that gets scrolled past and content that gets engagement.

Common Mistakes and How to Fix Them

Mistake: Being too vague. Bad: *"Help me with my business."* Good: *"I run an online store selling handmade candles. Sales have been flat for three months. Give me five marketing strategies I can implement this week with zero budget."*

Mistake: Asking for too much at once. Bad: *"Write a complete marketing plan, including brand strategy, social media calendar, email campaigns, SEO plan, and budget allocation."* Good: Ask for each piece separately. Start with the brand strategy, review it, then move to the social media calendar.

Mistake: Not specifying the audience. Bad: *"Explain machine learning."* Good: *"Explain machine learning to a small business owner who's considering using it for customer predictions. No technical jargon."*

Mistake: Accepting the first response. The first response is a draft, not the final answer. Iterate: *"Good, but make it shorter"* or *"Add more specific examples"* or *"That's too formal — make it conversational."*

Mistake: Over-engineering prompts. Simple tasks don't need elaborate prompt engineering. *"What's a good recipe for chocolate chip cookies?"* doesn't need a role, context, format, and constraints. Save structured prompting for tasks where precision matters.

Mistake: Not iterating. Many people write one prompt, get a response they don't love, and conclude ChatGPT isn't good at that task. The first response is almost always improvable with follow-ups. Treat your first prompt as a starting point, not a final attempt. *"That's close, but I need it more concise and with a stronger opening"* is often all it takes to go from a B response to an A.

Mistake: Writing prompts like search queries. *"best project management tools 2026 comparison"* is a search query, not a prompt. ChatGPT works better with natural language: *"I'm looking for a project management tool for a team of 12. We do software development with two-week sprints. What are the best options and how do they compare?"* The conversational version gives ChatGPT context to personalize the answer. The keyword version gets a generic list.

Mistake: Providing too much context. The opposite of vague is burying ChatGPT in a wall of text. At 500 words, ChatGPT may lose the thread of what you actually want. Front-load the most important information: start with what you need, then add context. *"Write a project update email. Context: we're three weeks into a six-week project..."* beats three paragraphs of background followed by "so can you write an email about this?"

Prompt Patterns That Work

The "Before and After" pattern: *"Here's my current version [paste text]. Here's what I want it to become [describe goal]. Transform it."*

The "Do This, Not That" pattern: *"Write a product description that's enthusiastic but not salesy, detailed but not overwhelming, professional but not stiff."*

The "Teach Me" pattern: *"Explain [concept] to me. Start with the simplest version, then add complexity. Stop me when it gets confusing."*

The "Challenge Me" pattern: *"Here's my plan [describe plan]. Find the weaknesses. What am I not thinking about? Where could this fail?"*

The "Step by Step" pattern: *"Walk me through [process] step by step. For each step, explain what to do, why it matters, and what could go wrong."*

The "Examples First" pattern: *"Here are three examples of the writing style I want [paste examples]. Now write [your request] in the same style."*

The "Iterate In Stages" pattern: *"Let's do this in three rounds. First, give me a rough draft. I'll give feedback. Then revise. Then we'll do a final polish."* Setting the expectation of iteration upfront changes how ChatGPT approaches the first draft — it takes more risks and gets more creative when it knows revision is built in.

The "Constraint Sandwich" pattern: *"Write a LinkedIn post about hiring mistakes. Constraints: under 150 words, no buzzwords, must include a specific example from a hiring process, end with a question. Tone: sharing a lesson with a friend over coffee."* Loading constraints around the task forces ChatGPT to be creative within boundaries — which often produces the most interesting output.

20 Prompt Templates for Everyday Use

1. *"Summarize [this text] in [number] bullet points."*
2. *"Write a [type] email to [recipient] about [topic]. Tone: [formal/casual/friendly]."*
3. *"Explain [concept] like I'm [age/expertise level]."*
4. *"Give me [number] ideas for [topic/goal]."*
5. *"Compare [option A] and [option B]. Which is better for [my situation]?"*
6. *"Create a [daily/weekly/monthly] plan for [goal]."*
7. *"Rewrite this to be [shorter/longer/more formal/simpler]: [text]."*
8. *"What questions should I ask about [topic/situation]?"*
9. *"Proofread this and fix any errors: [text]."*
10. *"Act as a [role]. [Question or task]."*
11. *"What are the pros and cons of [decision]?"*
12. *"Translate this to [language]: [text]."*
13. *"Create a table comparing [items] on [criteria]."*
14. *"Help me prepare for [event/meeting/interview]."*
15. *"Write a [social media post/blog outline/script] about [topic]."*
16. *"What's wrong with this [text/plan/approach]? How can I improve it?"*

17. *"Give me a step-by-step guide to [task]."*
18. *"I'm stuck on [problem]. Help me think through it."*
19. *"Draft a response to this [email/message]: [paste original]."*
20. *"Create a [budget/schedule/checklist] for [project/event]."*

These templates work because they're specific about the task, imply the format, and are easy to customize with your details.

The Meta-Prompt: When You Don't Know What to Ask

Sometimes you want help with something but can't frame the request. The meta-prompt:

"I'm trying to improve my team's weekly meetings. They run over time, people check out halfway through, and we rarely reach decisions. I'm not sure what to ask you. What questions should I answer so you can help me fix this?"

ChatGPT will ask targeted questions — how many people attend, what the agenda looks like, how decisions are made, who facilitates. By answering, you co-create the context that produces a useful response. This works best when the problem is complex enough that you don't know where to start.

Building Prompting Intuition Over Time

Prompting improves with practice. The more you use ChatGPT, the sharper your intuition for what produces great results. After a few weeks of active use, you'll notice patterns: you'll instinctively include context, you'll know when a role improves the output, you'll start follow-ups faster because you recognize what's missing.

A useful exercise: after every particularly good ChatGPT interaction, take ten seconds to note what made your prompt effective. The specificity? The role? The example you provided? Over time, these notes become your personal prompting playbook — not generic tips from a guide, but patterns that work specifically for your use cases.

The Honest Take on "Prompt Engineering"

You may have seen articles, courses, and job postings about "prompt engineering" — the idea that there's a deep technical skill to writing effective prompts. The truth: for most people using ChatGPT for everyday tasks, prompt engineering is overthinking it.

The principles in this chapter — be specific, give context, specify format, iterate — cover 95% of what you need. You don't need elaborate prompt frameworks or special syntax. You need to communicate clearly, just like you would with a capable human assistant.

Prompting skill genuinely matters on the margins: getting ChatGPT to produce output that's 90% right instead of 70% right on the first try. That difference matters when you're producing a lot of content or when the first draft needs to be close to final. But it's a refinement of communication skills you already have, not a new technical discipline.

The best prompters aren't prompt engineers — they're clear thinkers who know what they want and can articulate it. If you can explain something clearly to a colleague, you can prompt ChatGPT effectively. The rest is practice.

In the next chapter, we'll tackle longer, more complex tasks.

Chapter 25: Working with Long and Complex Tasks

Not everything fits in a single prompt. Some tasks are too big, too nuanced, or too multi-faceted for one shot. This chapter covers how to break down complex work and manage conversations that span dozens of exchanges.

Breaking Big Tasks into Steps

The most common mistake with complex tasks is trying to do everything at once. ChatGPT works better — and so do you — when you decompose a large task into manageable steps.

Instead of: *"Write a complete business plan for my startup."*

Try: 1. *"Help me define my value proposition. My startup does [X] for [Y]. Challenge my thinking."* 2. *"Based on our discussion, draft the executive summary section."* 3. *"Now let's work on the market analysis. Here's what I know about the market: [details]."* 4. *"Draft the competitive analysis. I know of these competitors: [list]."* 5. *"Let's build the financial projections. Help me think through the assumptions first."*

Each step produces better output because ChatGPT can focus. And you can review and correct each piece before building on it.

Why this works so much better: When you ask ChatGPT to do everything at once, it makes hundreds of decisions simultaneously: what to include, what to leave out, how much depth, what tone, what format. Many of those decisions will be wrong for your needs. Break it into steps and you make those decisions together, one at a time. You approve the value proposition before moving to the financial model. You refine the executive summary before drafting the competitive analysis. Each step builds on a reviewed foundation rather than a tower of unchecked assumptions.

A concrete example: Ask ChatGPT to "write a 5-page marketing strategy for a new fitness app." You'll get something that looks comprehensive but is full of assumptions you'd never make — wrong audience, wrong pricing tier, wrong competitive positioning. Now try step-by-step: (1) define the target audience with ChatGPT, (2) analyze the competitive landscape, (3) agree on positioning, (4) develop the channel strategy, (5) build the budget. The final product is dramatically better because every foundation was checked before building on it.

Chaining Prompts

Prompt chaining is the technique of using the output of one prompt as the input for the next:

1. *"Brainstorm 20 blog post ideas about remote work."*
2. *"Pick the five most original ideas from that list and write a one-paragraph pitch for each."*
3. *"Take idea #3 and create a detailed outline."*
4. *"Write the first draft based on that outline."*
5. *"Now edit it for conciseness and add a stronger opening."*

Each prompt builds on the previous response, creating a pipeline that progressively refines the output. This beats a single prompt asking for the finished product.

Managing Context in Long Conversations

As covered in Chapter 5, ChatGPT has a context window — a limit on how much conversation it can "see" at once. In long conversations, that becomes a practical concern.

Signs you're losing context: - ChatGPT contradicts something it said earlier - It forgets constraints you set ("I told you to keep it under 500 words") - It asks you something you've already answered - The quality of responses drops or becomes more generic

Strategies for managing long conversations:

Restate key constraints. Every 10–15 messages, remind ChatGPT of the important parameters: *"Remember, we're writing this for a technical audience, formal tone, each section under 300 words."*

Summarize progress. Ask ChatGPT to summarize what you've established so far: *"Before we continue, summarize the key decisions we've made in this conversation."* This refreshes the context.

Use "so far" recaps. Start new stages with a brief recap: *"So far we've completed the introduction and chapters 1-3. The thesis is [X], the tone is [Y], the target audience is [Z]. Now let's start chapter 4."*

Reference by name. If you've created specific outputs earlier, reference them by name rather than assuming ChatGPT remembers: *"Using the pricing framework we created earlier (the three-tier model), draft the pricing page copy."*

Create explicit checkpoints. At key moments, ask ChatGPT to summarize the state of the work: *"Before we continue, list everything we've decided so far: target audience, key messages, format, constraints."* This creates a reference point you can paste back in if context drifts. Think of checkpoints as save points in a video game — they let you restore the state if things go off track.

Use Projects for long-term complex work. If a task spans multiple conversations over multiple days, create a Project (Chapter 19) and put the key context — goals, constraints, decisions, completed drafts — in the Project instructions or uploaded files. Each new conversation starts with the full context already loaded.

When to Start Fresh

Sometimes the best strategy is a new conversation:

- **The conversation has become unwieldy** — You've gone down several wrong paths and the context is cluttered with abandoned approaches
- **You're switching phases** — Research is done and you're starting to write
- **Quality is degrading** — Responses are turning generic or contradictory
- **You want a clean perspective** — Starting fresh means ChatGPT approaches the problem without the assumptions built up in the current conversation

When starting fresh, bring forward the essential context:

"I've been working on a business proposal in another conversation. Here's what we established: [key decisions and context]. Now I need to draft the executive summary based on these points."

Multi-Session Projects

For truly large projects — a book, a course curriculum, a comprehensive research project — you'll work across multiple conversations over days or weeks. This is where Projects (Chapter 19) become essential.

1. **Create a Project** with clear instructions and reference files
2. **Start each conversation** with a brief statement of what you're working on in this session
3. **Save key outputs** (outlines, decisions, completed sections) as files within the project
4. **Reference previous work** by uploading completed sections when starting new ones

This maintains continuity across sessions without relying on ChatGPT to remember everything from previous conversations.

Techniques for Complex Reasoning

When the task requires careful thinking — not just retrieval but actual reasoning — these techniques help:

"Think step by step." Adding this phrase genuinely improves reasoning quality: *"Think step by step about how we should price this product."*

"Consider multiple perspectives." *"Analyze this decision from the perspective of the customer, the sales team, and the engineering team."*

"What am I missing?" After ChatGPT provides an analysis, ask this. It often surfaces considerations the initial response skipped.

"Argue the other side." If ChatGPT recommends option A, ask it to make the strongest case for option B. This stress-tests the recommendation.

"What would need to be true?" Instead of "Will this work?", ask "What would need to be true for this to work?" Produces more actionable analysis.

Use GPT-5.4 Thinking for complex reasoning. On Plus or Pro, when working through a genuinely complex problem, switch to it. The reasoning quality difference is significant on hard tasks.

"Steelman, then attack." Ask ChatGPT to make the strongest possible case for an idea, then follow up: *"Now tear that apart. What are the fatal flaws?"* This two-step approach produces more balanced analysis than asking for pros and cons in one prompt, because each step gets ChatGPT's full attention.

The "rubber duck" technique. Sometimes the value isn't in ChatGPT's response but in your own thinking. Explain your problem to ChatGPT in detail — constraints, options, what you've tried, what's not working. Many people find the act of explaining the problem clearly reveals the solution before ChatGPT even responds. Programmers call this "rubber duck debugging," and it works just as well for business problems, personal decisions, and creative blocks.

Common Patterns for Complex Work

Different types of complex tasks call for different approaches:

Writing a long document: Outline → Chapter by chapter → Consistency review → Final polish. Never try to generate the whole thing at once.

Making a complex decision: Gather information → List options → Analyze each → Stress-test the top choice → Decide. Use ChatGPT for each phase separately.

Learning a new subject: Overview → Key concepts → Deep dive on each concept → Practice problems → Self-assessment. Progressive depth, not all-at-once.

Building something (a plan, a product, a strategy): Define requirements → Draft the structure → Build each component → Review the whole → Iterate.

The common thread: decompose, execute in stages, review between stages. This isn't just good prompting — it's good thinking. ChatGPT makes it faster, but the discipline of breaking work into stages is a human skill that makes AI assistance dramatically more effective.

Walkthrough: Writing a 10-Page Business Proposal

Let's put these techniques together on a substantial real-world task.

Session 1 — Research and framework (20 minutes): 1. *"I need to write a business proposal for implementing a customer loyalty program at our mid-size e-commerce company. Before we write anything, help me think through the key questions: What do we need to decide? What data do we need? Who's the audience?"* 2. Review ChatGPT's framework. Add your specific context. 3. *"Search the web for current data on customer loyalty program ROI for e-commerce companies. Focus on 2025-2026 data."* 4. *"Based on our discussion, create a detailed outline for a 10-page proposal. The audience is our CEO and CFO."*

Session 2 — First draft, sections 1–3 (30 minutes): 5. Start a new conversation in the same Project. Paste the outline. 6. *"Draft the Executive Summary based on our outline. This is the most important section — it needs to be compelling enough to make the CEO want to read the rest."* 7. Review, refine, approve. 8. *"Draft the Market Context section. Use the research data we gathered."* 9. *"Draft the Proposed Program Design section."*

Session 3 — Remaining sections and polish (30 minutes): 10. Continue with the financial analysis, implementation plan, and risk assessment sections. 11. *"Read through the full proposal. Check for consistency in tone, logical flow between sections, and any contradictions. List what needs fixing."* 12. Fix the identified issues. 13. *"Write a strong closing section that summarizes the ask and creates urgency."*

Total time: about 80 minutes across three sessions. The result is a polished, data-backed, professionally structured proposal that would have taken a day or more from scratch.

The key technique: never try to write the whole thing in one shot. Research first. Outline second. Draft in sections. Review the whole. Polish last. Each step builds on a checked foundation.

In the next chapter, we cover the last piece of the skills puzzle: controlling the format and presentation of ChatGPT's output.

Chapter 26: Output Formatting and Control

Getting the right information from ChatGPT is only half the battle. Getting it in the right format — the structure, length, and presentation that matches your needs — is the other half. This chapter covers how to control what ChatGPT's responses look like.

Requesting Specific Formats

ChatGPT can produce output in virtually any text format. Just ask:

Tables: *"Present this comparison as a table with columns for Product, Price, Rating, and Key Feature."*

Bullet points: *"Give me the key takeaways as bullet points, not paragraphs."*

Numbered lists: *"List the steps in order."*

Headers and sections: *"Structure this with clear section headers."*

Q&A format: *"Present this as a FAQ — list the most common questions with brief answers."*

Email format: *"Format this as a ready-to-send email with subject line, greeting, body, and sign-off."*

JSON/structured data: *"Return the results as a JSON object."*

Markdown: *"Format this in Markdown with proper headers, bold, and code blocks."*

Plain text: *"Give me this as plain text with no formatting — no bold, no bullets, no headers. Just clean paragraphs."*

Conversational: *"Don't format this at all. Just explain it to me like we're talking."*

ChatGPT's defaults vs. what you probably want: Left alone, ChatGPT loves bullet points, bold headers, and structured lists. Great for reference material; robotic for email drafts, social posts, and casual communication. If you want something that reads like a human wrote it, ask for prose: *"Write this in flowing paragraphs, not bullet points."* The output sounds dramatically more natural.

Controlling Length

Length is one of the most common formatting requests:

"Keep it under 100 words." "Write exactly three paragraphs." "Give me the one-sentence version." "Write a detailed, comprehensive response — don't worry about length." "Two bullet points per section, maximum."

ChatGPT approximates length — if you ask for 100 words, you might get 85 or 120. For exact length, count and ask for adjustments: *"That was 150 words. Cut it to 100 without losing the key points."*

The honest take on length control: ChatGPT handles relative instructions ("make it shorter," "give me the brief version," "expand this") better than absolute numbers ("exactly 200 words"). If you need around 200 words, say "about 200 words." If you have a hard constraint — a Twitter/X post under 280 characters, an abstract under 150 words for a conference submission — provide the limit and have ChatGPT check itself: *"Write a conference abstract under 150 words. After writing it, count the words and confirm it's within the limit."*

A length trick for long documents: When you need a longer piece and ChatGPT comes in short, try: *"Good start, but I need at least 2,000 words. Expand each section with more examples, more detail, more practical advice. Don't pad with filler — add genuine depth."* The last sentence matters. Without it, ChatGPT will sometimes add fluffy transitions and redundant rephrasing to hit the word count rather than adding substance.

Getting Consistent Output

When you need multiple outputs to follow the same pattern (a series of product descriptions, a batch of social media posts, chapter summaries), establish the pattern first:

Step 1: Create or approve one example. **Step 2:** Tell ChatGPT to use it as a template: *"Follow this exact format for the remaining items."* **Step 3:** Generate the rest.

If consistency drifts over a long session, paste the template again: *"Here's the format to follow. Apply it to the next batch."*

For batch output: When generating multiple items in a consistent format — product descriptions, email templates, social posts — the template approach is essential:

1. Write one example yourself (or approve ChatGPT's first draft)
2. Tell ChatGPT: *"This is the template. Match this format, tone, and length exactly."*
3. Ask for the next batch: *"Generate 5 more, following the same template."*
4. Review and refine.

This produces far more consistent output than asking for all items at once. The template gives ChatGPT a concrete example to match, not just instructions to interpret.

Tone Control

Formal: *"Write this in a professional, formal tone suitable for a board presentation."* **Casual:** *"Make it conversational, like you're explaining to a friend."* **Technical:** *"Use precise technical language. The audience is engineers."* **Simple:** *"Write this at a sixth-grade reading level."* **Persuasive:** *"Make this compelling. I need to convince stakeholders to approve the budget."* **Neutral:** *"Present both sides equally without taking a position."*

You can also reference specific styles: *"Write like a New York Times feature article"* or *"Match the tone of this example: [paste sample]."*

Combining tone and format for specific contexts:

For a team Slack message: "Write this as a brief Slack message. Casual but professional. One or two short paragraphs max."

For a client presentation: "Write this as speaker notes for a slide deck. Each section should be 2-3 sentences that I can read naturally while presenting."

For an internal wiki: "Write this as documentation. Third person, present tense, step-by-step instructions. Assume the reader knows nothing about this process."

For a personal blog: "Write this in a first-person, storytelling style. Start with an anecdote. Make it feel like I'm telling a friend about what happened."

Destination determines format. Tell ChatGPT both the tone and the medium and the output arrives ready to use rather than requiring reformatting.

Exporting and Sharing

ChatGPT responses can be used in several ways:

Copy and paste. The simplest approach — copy the text and paste it into your document, email, or app. On desktop, Ctrl+C / Cmd+C works on the entire response or on selected text. ChatGPT's responses are formatted in Markdown, so when pasting into apps that understand Markdown (Notion, Slack, many email clients), the formatting — bold, headers, bullet points — comes through correctly. In plain-text environments, the Markdown symbols (**bold**, # headers) may appear as raw text. Fix: *"Reformat this as plain text without any Markdown."*

Download files. When ChatGPT creates spreadsheets, documents, or other files through Code Interpreter, it provides download links. These expire, so download anything important promptly.

Share conversations. Generate a shareable link to a conversation, letting others read (but not edit) the exchange.

Export all data. Settings lets you request a full export of all your conversations.

Handling Output You Don't Want

Knowing how to correct formatting is as important as requesting it:

"Don't use bullet points — write in flowing paragraphs." "Stop adding disclaimers at the end of your responses." "Don't start every paragraph with a bold header." "Less formal — you're being too stiff." "Stop saying 'Great question!' Just answer."

ChatGPT has default formatting habits (it loves bullet points, bold headers, and preamble). If those habits don't match your needs, tell it to stop. These corrections can also go in your Custom Instructions so you don't repeat them.

The most common formatting annoyances (and how to fix them):

Annoying habit	Fix
Starting with "Great question!" or "Absolutely!"	*"Skip the preamble. Just answer."*
Adding unnecessary disclaimers at the end	*"Don't add disclaimers or caveats."*
Over-using bold headers for short responses	*"Write in plain prose, no headers."*
Padding responses with filler sentences	*"Be concise. Every sentence should add information."*
Using corporate jargon	*"Write in plain English. No buzzwords."*
Bullet-pointing everything	*"Use paragraphs, not bullet points."*
Hedging every statement	*"Be direct. Commit to your recommendations."*

Put your top three in Custom Instructions and you'll eliminate most formatting friction across all conversations.

Walkthrough: Formatting for Multiple Destinations

Imagine you've written a product announcement with ChatGPT. Now you need it in four different formats:

1. *"Format this as an email announcement to our customer list. Subject line, greeting, three paragraphs, and a CTA button."*
2. *"Now format the same announcement as a LinkedIn post. Under 200 words, professional tone, end with a question."*
3. *"Create a version for our internal Slack channel. Casual, brief, with relevant emoji."*

4. *"Finally, format it as a press release. Standard AP style, include a boilerplate about our company."*

Same content, four formats, each appropriate for its destination. Far more efficient than rewriting from scratch for each channel.

Formatting for Specific Destinations

Different destinations have different formatting needs:

For email: *"Format this as a ready-to-send email. Include a subject line."*

For presentations: *"Create this as slide-by-slide content. For each slide, give me: a title, three bullet points, and speaker notes."*

For social media: *"Write this as a LinkedIn post. Keep it under 200 words. End with a question to drive engagement."*

For documentation: *"Format this as technical documentation with clear sections, code examples, and notes."*

For print: *"Format this for print. Use complete sentences, no markdown formatting, and traditional paragraph structure."*

The key insight: don't adapt ChatGPT's output after the fact. Tell ChatGPT what you need upfront and it produces output ready to use with minimal modification.

Putting Formatting Into Custom Instructions

If you find yourself making the same formatting requests repeatedly — "don't use bullet points," "keep it under 200 words," "use markdown tables for comparisons" — put those in your Custom Instructions (Settings, then Personalization, then Custom Instructions). Every conversation starts with your preferred defaults.

A well-tuned Custom Instructions profile eliminates 80% of formatting corrections. Instead of saying "don't start with a greeting" in every conversation, you say it once and it applies everywhere. The remaining 20% are situation-specific — and those are the ones worth typing each time.

A formatting cheat sheet to save:

You want...	Say...
No AI-sounding preamble	"Skip the preamble. Just answer."
Shorter responses	"Be concise. Three sentences max."
More depth	"Go deep on this. Don't hold back on detail."
Tables	"Compare these in a table."
Ready-to-use output	"Format this as a ready-to-send email."
No bullet points	"Write in flowing prose, not lists."
Specific word count	"Keep it to about [N] words."
Multiple formats	"Give me three versions: formal, casual, and brief."

Part VII: ChatGPT for Your World

"Technology is nothing. What's important is that you have a faith in people, that they're basically good and smart, and if you give them tools, they'll do wonderful things with them."

— Steve Jobs

Chapter 27: ChatGPT for Students and Educators

ChatGPT is transforming education — for better and worse. This chapter covers how students can use it as a genuine learning tool (not a shortcut machine) and how educators can put it to work for teaching.

For Students: ChatGPT as a Tutor

The most valuable way to use ChatGPT as a student is as a personal tutor — available 24/7, infinitely patient, able to explain any concept at any level.

Study Mode and Interactive Learning

We covered Study Mode and Interactive Learning in Chapter 7. Here's what matters specifically for students:

Study Mode turns ChatGPT from an answer machine into a tutor. Instead of giving you the answer, it asks *you* questions to figure out what you already understand, then builds from there. The difference between looking up an answer (which you'll forget) and actually learning (which sticks).

"I have an organic chemistry exam in three days. Use Study Mode to help me review nucleophilic substitution reactions. Start by assessing what I know."

Interactive Learning makes abstract concepts tangible. For the 70+ math and science topics that support it, you can manipulate variables and watch results change in real time. Especially valuable for subjects where students struggle with the "why" behind formulas — seeing the Pythagorean theorem respond to changing inputs builds intuition that memorizing $a^2 + b^2 = c^2$ never will.

The key student strategy: Use Study Mode for exam prep at least a week before the test, not the night before. Its strength is building understanding through repeated interaction, not last-minute cramming.

How Study Mode differs from just asking questions: In regular ChatGPT, ask "What is mitosis?" and you get an explanation. In Study Mode, you might get: "Before I explain it, tell me what you already know about cell division." Based on your answer, it calibrates the explanation. Then: "Can you explain the four stages of mitosis in your own words?" If you get stage three wrong, it corrects you and asks you to try again. This back-and-forth is what makes Study Mode an actual learning tool rather than a fancy encyclopedia. The research on learning is clear: retrieval practice (being asked to recall information) produces far stronger learning than passive reading. Study Mode automates retrieval practice.

Using ChatGPT to Study Effectively

Concept explanations: *"Explain the difference between mitosis and meiosis. Use an analogy to help me remember."*

Practice problems: *"Give me five practice problems on integration by parts. Start easy and get harder. Don't show solutions until I ask."*

Exam prep: *"I have a US History exam on the Civil War era. Create a practice exam with 15 questions — mix of multiple choice, short answer, and one essay question."*

Paper research: *"I'm writing a paper on the impact of social media on teenage mental health. Help me identify the key arguments on both sides and suggest search terms for finding academic sources."*

Peer review: *"Read my essay draft and give me feedback. Focus on argument structure and evidence quality, not grammar: [paste text]."*

Office hours substitute: *"I'm stuck on problem 7 of my thermodynamics homework. Here's the problem [paste it]. Don't solve it for me. Instead, give me a hint about which concept I should apply and ask me a question that will help me figure out the approach."*

This is the ChatGPT equivalent of going to office hours. The key phrase is "don't solve it for me" — it keeps ChatGPT in coaching mode rather than answer mode. A genuinely effective way to get unstuck without shortcutting the learning.

Language learning: *"I'm learning French at a B1 level. Have a conversation with me entirely in French. Use vocabulary appropriate for my level. If I make a* *grammar mistake, gently correct it in parentheses, then continue the conversation."*

ChatGPT is an infinitely patient conversation partner for language learning. Unlike a human tutor, it's available at 2 AM, never tires of your mistakes, and adjusts to your exact level in real time. Advanced Voice Mode makes it even more powerful — you can practice pronunciation, not just grammar.

The "explain it back" technique: After studying a concept, try: *"I'm going to explain [concept] to you. Listen to my explanation and then tell me: (1) what I got right, (2) what I got wrong, (3) what I left out."* This forces you to articulate your understanding — one of the most effective study techniques. ChatGPT acts as a patient audience that gives honest feedback.

Codex for Students

Verified university students in the US and Canada can claim $100 in credits for Codex, OpenAI's agentic coding tool. If you're in a CS program or any field that involves programming, this is worth applying for.

For Educators: ChatGPT as a Teaching Tool

Lesson Planning

"Create a 50-minute lesson plan for high school biology on the water cycle. Include a warm-up activity, main instruction, a group activity, and an assessment. Assume students have no prior knowledge."

"I'm teaching a college-level creative writing workshop. Design a 90-minute session on writing dialogue. Include examples from published fiction and a writing exercise."

Creating Materials

"Generate a worksheet with 20 vocabulary words related to the American Revolution. Include definitions, context sentences, and a matching exercise."

"Create a rubric for grading argumentative essays. Categories should include: thesis statement, evidence quality, counterargument, organization, and writing mechanics."

"Design a group project for my eighth-grade science class on renewable energy. It should take two weeks and result in a presentation."

Differentiation

"Rewrite this reading passage at three different levels: below grade level, at grade level, and above grade level. Keep the core content the same."

"Create a version of this math assignment with scaffolding for students who struggle with fractions."

Generating examples from student life: *"I'm teaching supply and demand to high school sophomores. Create five examples using things they actually care about: concert tickets, sneakers, video games, streaming services, and fast food."*

ChatGPT translates abstract concepts into examples that resonate with your specific student population. This kind of contextual example generation is one of the most time-consuming parts of lesson planning, and ChatGPT does it in seconds.

Creating answer keys and rubrics: *"Here's the quiz I created [paste it]. Generate a detailed answer key with explanations for each answer. Also note common mistakes students make on each question."*

The "common mistakes" addition is invaluable for anticipating where students will struggle and writing feedback that addresses their actual misunderstandings, not just marking answers wrong.

Assessment

"Create a quiz on Chapter 5 of To Kill a Mockingbird. Include comprehension, analysis, and one creative response question."

"Generate five essay prompts about the causes of World War I that test different levels of Bloom's taxonomy."

Academic Integrity

This is the most important section in this chapter. The line between using ChatGPT as a learning tool and using it to cheat is sometimes clear and sometimes blurry.

Clearly appropriate: - Using ChatGPT to explain a concept you don't understand - Getting feedback on a draft you wrote yourself - Generating practice problems for studying - Having ChatGPT quiz you on material - Using it to outline ideas before writing

Clearly inappropriate: - Submitting ChatGPT's output as your own work (unless explicitly permitted) - Having ChatGPT write your essays, homework, or exam answers - Using it during closed-book assessments - Presenting AI-generated research as your own research

The gray area: - Using ChatGPT to improve your writing (Where does editing end and ghostwriting begin?) - Using it for brainstorming (Is the idea yours if ChatGPT suggested it?) - Using it for coding assignments (Is the code yours if you prompted it?)

The answer to gray-area questions depends on your institution's policies, your professor's expectations, and your own ethical judgment. When in doubt:

1. **Read your institution's AI policy.** Most schools now have explicit guidelines.
2. **Ask your professor.** They'll appreciate the honesty.
3. **Disclose your use.** If you used ChatGPT in any meaningful way, say so.
4. **Ask yourself:** Did I learn the material, or did I outsource the learning?

The purpose of education is learning, not producing deliverables. ChatGPT is an extraordinary learning tool when used to deepen understanding. It's counterproductive when used to bypass it.

A practical test for students: Before using ChatGPT for an assignment, ask: "If my professor asked me to explain this topic without notes, could I?" If no, use ChatGPT to learn the topic first, then do the assignment yourself. If you use ChatGPT to write the assignment without understanding the material, you get the grade but miss the education — and the gap shows up on exams, in class discussions, and eventually in your career.

A note for educators: Students who use ChatGPT as a learning accelerator — to understand concepts more deeply, to get unstuck, to practice skills — will outperform students who don't use it at all. Students who use ChatGPT as a shortcut to avoid learning will fall behind. The challenge for educators is creating assessments and learning environments that reward understanding over output, making the learning-accelerator approach the obviously better strategy.

Age-Appropriate Use

For younger users:

- OpenAI requires users to be at least 13 years old (18 in some regions)
- Parents should be aware of what their children are using ChatGPT for
- ChatGPT has safety filters for age-inappropriate content, but they're not perfect
- Younger students should use ChatGPT with parental awareness and, ideally, some supervision
- Teaching children to use AI responsibly is a skill as important as teaching them to use the internet responsibly

Walkthroughs: Student and Educator in Action

Student walkthrough — Preparing for a midterm:

1. *"I have a psychology midterm covering chapters 4-8 of my textbook. The topics are memory, learning theory, motivation, emotion, and social psychology. Start by quizzing me on key concepts from memory (chapter 4). Ask one question at a time."*
2. Answer the question. ChatGPT gives you feedback and explains what you got wrong.
3. After 10 questions: *"Based on my answers, which concepts do I need to study more?"*
4. ChatGPT identifies your weak areas. You focus your remaining study time there.
5. *"Create a one-page summary sheet covering all five topics. Highlight the concepts I got wrong."*
6. Use the summary sheet for final review.

Dramatically more effective than re-reading the textbook or reviewing highlighted notes. You're actively testing yourself, identifying gaps, and focusing effort where it matters most.

Educator walkthrough — Differentiating a lesson:

1. *"I'm teaching the water cycle to a 5th grade class. Three of my students are English language learners, five are below grade level in reading, and two are advanced. Create three versions of my lesson handout: (1) a simplified version with more visuals and shorter sentences for ELL and below-grade-level students, (2) a standard version for grade-level students, and (3) an enrichment version for advanced students that introduces the concept of evapotranspiration."*
2. Review all three versions. Adjust as needed.
3. *"Now create a quick assessment (5 questions) that all three groups can take, with the first three questions assessing basic understanding and the last two assessing deeper comprehension."*

What used to take an hour of careful rewriting takes about 15 minutes with ChatGPT. The time saved goes into what technology can't replace: connecting with students individually.

ChatGPT in education isn't going away. The students and educators who thrive will be those who use it as a tool for deeper learning rather than a shortcut around it.

In the next chapter, we look at how businesses and teams can use ChatGPT effectively and responsibly.

Chapter 28: ChatGPT for Business and Teams

ChatGPT is becoming standard business infrastructure, like email and spreadsheets. This chapter covers how organizations can deploy and use ChatGPT effectively, from small teams to large enterprises.

Team Workspaces

Business and Enterprise plans provide shared workspaces where teams can:

- Share Custom GPTs built for internal use
- Maintain consistent AI usage across the organization
- Centralize billing and user management
- Enforce data privacy and security policies

A team workspace means everyone has access to the same tools, Custom GPTs, and configurations — without managing individual accounts.

What this looks like in practice: Your marketing team has a Custom GPT called "Brand Voice Checker" with your style guide uploaded that reviews copy for brand consistency. With a team workspace, everyone on the team can access it without building their own version. The admin sets it up once, and it's available to all team members. This alone saves hours of duplicated effort — and more importantly, it ensures everyone is using the same reference material and standards.

The honest case for Business over individual Plus accounts: If three or more people on your team are using personal Plus accounts for work, switching to Business is almost always the right move. You get data privacy guarantees (no training on your conversations), centralized billing (one invoice instead of multiple expense reports), admin controls, and higher message limits. At $25/user/month versus $20/user for Plus, the $5 premium pays for itself in governance alone.

Use Cases by Department

Marketing

- Content creation: blog posts, social media, ad copy, email campaigns
- Market research: competitive analysis, trend identification, audience insights
- SEO: keyword research, content optimization, meta descriptions
- Brand voice: create a Custom GPT that enforces your brand guidelines

Sales

- Prospect research: quickly learn about companies before calls
- Email drafting: personalized outreach at scale
- Proposal writing: first drafts of proposals and RFP responses
- CRM data analysis: upload CRM exports for pipeline analysis
- Objection handling: practice responses to common objections

Human Resources

- Job descriptions: draft role descriptions consistent with company standards
- Interview preparation: generate interview questions tailored to specific roles
- Policy drafting: create first drafts of HR policies
- Employee communications: draft announcements, memos, and FAQs
- Onboarding: build an onboarding GPT that answers new hire questions

Operations

- Process documentation: turn messy process knowledge into clear SOPs
- Meeting efficiency: create agendas, summarize notes, track action items
- Vendor evaluation: compare vendor proposals systematically
- Report generation: create regular reports from data uploads

Customer Support

- Response drafting: generate customer-facing responses in your brand voice

- Knowledge base: build a GPT trained on your product documentation
- Escalation support: help agents research complex customer issues
- Quality analysis: analyze support ticket data for trends and improvement opportunities

Quick wins by department:

Marketing: Build a brand voice GPT with your style guide, tone examples, and messaging framework uploaded. Every piece of content starts on-brand instead of requiring multiple revision rounds.

Sales: Build a "Deal Prep" GPT that takes a company name and produces a brief on the business, recent news, likely pain points, and suggested talking points. Reps spend five minutes prepping for calls instead of thirty.

HR: Build a "Policy Q&A" GPT with your employee handbook uploaded. It answers routine questions ("How many vacation days do I get?" "What's our parental leave policy?") instantly and accurately, cutting HR inbox volume.

Operations: Use ChatGPT to turn tribal knowledge into documented SOPs. Have the person who knows the process explain it to ChatGPT, then ask ChatGPT to write it up as a formal, step-by-step procedure. Review, refine, publish. Captures institutional knowledge that would otherwise live only in people's heads.

Data Governance

The most important consideration for business use is data privacy. Understanding how your data flows is critical:

Free, Go, and Plus plans: - Conversations may be used for model training (unless opted out) - Not suitable for sensitive business data

Business plan: - Data is not used for model training - Admin controls for user management - Suitable for most business use cases

Enterprise plan: - Data is not used for model training - Advanced security: SSO, audit logs, compliance certifications - Custom data retention policies - Required for regulated industries (healthcare, finance, legal)

A critical distinction for decision-makers: The difference between Business and Enterprise isn't just features — it's risk. Business provides data privacy and centralized management, sufficient for most companies. Enterprise adds compliance certifications (SOC 2, HIPAA eligibility), SSO integration, custom data retention, and audit capabilities that regulated industries require. If your company handles customer health records, financial data, or legal case files, Enterprise isn't a luxury — it's a requirement. If you're a marketing agency or a software consultancy, Business is almost certainly sufficient.

Building an AI Usage Policy

Every organization using ChatGPT should have a clear AI usage policy. Here's a framework:

Allowed uses: - List specific, approved use cases - Specify which plans/tools are approved

Prohibited uses: - No sharing of customer personal data - No sharing of trade secrets or proprietary code - No sharing of confidential financial information - No using AI output as final decisions without human review

Disclosure requirements: - When and how employees should disclose AI use - Which deliverables require disclosure

Quality standards: - All AI-generated content must be reviewed by a human - AI outputs should be fact-checked before publication - Critical communications should not be fully AI-generated

Training: - All employees should complete AI literacy training - Department-specific training on relevant use cases - Regular updates as capabilities and policies evolve

Admin Controls

Business and Enterprise admins can:

- Manage which users have access
- Control which features are available
- Monitor usage patterns (not conversation content)
- Enable or disable specific connectors
- Set data retention policies

- Configure SSO and authentication
- Review audit logs for compliance purposes (Enterprise)

What admins can't do: On Business and Enterprise plans, admins see usage patterns (who's using ChatGPT, how often, which features) but cannot read employees' conversations. This is deliberate privacy protection — your company knows you used ChatGPT at 2 PM for 15 minutes, but not what you discussed. It matters for employee trust: people use ChatGPT more freely (and therefore more productively) when they know their conversations are private.

ROI Considerations

Quantifying ChatGPT's business value:

Time savings: Track time saved on common tasks. A marketing team of five saving 3 hours per person per week is 60 hours per month.

Quality improvement: AI-assisted work is often more thorough and consistent than unassisted work, especially for research and analysis.

Capability expansion: Tasks that previously required specialized skills or external contractors can sometimes be handled internally.

Employee satisfaction: Removing tedious tasks and providing a powerful assistant improves job satisfaction and cuts burnout.

Against costs: - Subscription fees ($25/user/month for Business) - Training time - Risks from misuse - Time spent reviewing AI output

For most knowledge-work organizations, the math is clear: ChatGPT at $25/user/month pays for itself if it saves each employee more than about 30 minutes per week. Most users save that in the first week.

Building the internal business case: To convince leadership to invest, pick three concrete, repeatable tasks your team does every week (writing reports, prepping for meetings, drafting client emails). Have 2–3 team members do those tasks with and without ChatGPT, and measure the time difference. Then extrapolate: if each person saves X hours per week, and your fully-loaded hourly cost is Y, annual savings is X * Y * 52 * number_of_users. This calculation almost always dwarfs the subscription cost. Present that math alongside a data privacy summary (Business plan, no training on data) and a proposed usage policy.

A measurement warning: Don't just measure time savings — track quality. Many organizations find ChatGPT-assisted work isn't just faster, it's more thorough. Reports cover more angles. Emails are better structured. Research is more comprehensive. The quality improvement is harder to quantify but often more valuable than the time savings.

Getting Started: A Practical Rollout Plan

If you're introducing ChatGPT to your organization:

1. **Start small.** Pick one team or department for a pilot. Marketing and customer support are common starting points — the use cases are clear and risks are low.
2. **Set guidelines first.** Write your AI usage policy before rolling out access, not after.
3. **Train your people.** Don't just hand out licenses. Run a 60-minute session covering basic prompting, privacy guidelines, and approved use cases.
4. **Collect feedback.** After two weeks, ask your pilot group what worked, what didn't, and what surprised them.
5. **Expand deliberately.** Roll out to additional teams based on what you learned from the pilot.
6. **Review quarterly.** AI capabilities change fast. Revisit your policy and training materials every quarter.

The organizations that get the most value from ChatGPT aren't the ones that adopt it fastest — they're the ones that adopt it most thoughtfully.

Common Mistakes in Business Adoption

Mistake: Giving everyone access without training. People who don't know how to prompt will get mediocre results, conclude ChatGPT isn't useful, and stop using it. Thirty minutes of basic training on prompting, privacy, and role-relevant use cases is the difference between adoption and abandonment.

Mistake: No clear policy on what can and can't be shared. Without guidelines, employees either share too much (proprietary data on personal accounts) or too little (refusing to use ChatGPT at all out of fear). A clear policy removes the ambiguity and gives people confidence to use the tool appropriately.

Mistake: Expecting immediate transformation. ChatGPT's value compounds as people develop better prompting skills, build Custom GPTs, and integrate it into workflows. First week, modest gains. First month, meaningful ones. First quarter, compounding returns. Set expectations accordingly — this is an investment in capability, not a switch you flip.

Mistake: Treating all departments the same. Marketing and customer support typically see the fastest ROI because their work is text-heavy and repetitive. Engineering teams may get more value from Codex than from ChatGPT proper. Finance teams may need specific data analysis training. Tailor rollout and training to each department's actual use cases rather than running generic training for everyone.

The next chapter covers ChatGPT for creators and freelancers — an audience that uses it as a competitive advantage.

Chapter 29: ChatGPT for Creators and Freelancers

If you create for a living — writing, design, video, photography, consulting, or any other creative or freelance work — ChatGPT can be your most versatile team member. Not a replacement for your creative vision, but a force multiplier for the parts of the job you'd rather not do.

Content Creation Workflows

The Content Machine

A typical workflow for a content creator using ChatGPT:

1. **Ideation:** *"Give me 20 video topic ideas for my YouTube channel about personal finance for millennials."*
2. **Research:** *"For topic #7, what are the key points I should cover? Search for recent data."*
3. **Outline:** *"Create a video script outline. Hook, three main sections, and a call to action."*
4. **Script:** *"Write the full script in a conversational, energetic tone. About 8 minutes of speaking."*
5. **Thumbnail:** *"Generate three thumbnail concepts for this video using DALL-E."*
6. **Description:** *"Write the YouTube description with timestamps, keywords, and a call to action."*
7. **Social promotion:** *"Create an X (formerly Twitter) thread, an Instagram caption, and a LinkedIn post to promote this video."*

What used to take a day of prep now takes an hour of ChatGPT-assisted work.

The meta-strategy most creators miss: Build a Project (Chapter 19) for your content work. Upload your brand guidelines, content calendar, examples of your best-performing posts, and audience demographics. Every new content conversation starts with this context loaded. Instead of explaining your brand, audience, and style every time, you say: *"Write next week's newsletter about [topic]"* and the Project context fills in the rest. Over time, this Project becomes your content operating system.

Repurposing Content

One of the most time-efficient strategies for creators is repurposing content across platforms:

"Here's my latest blog post [paste text]. Create: (1) An X thread summarizing the key points, (2) Three LinkedIn posts pulling different angles, (3) An email newsletter version, and (4) Five Instagram carousel slide ideas."

ChatGPT understands each platform's conventions and adapts accordingly.

A repurposing prompt that works for any content: *"Here's a [blog post / podcast transcript / YouTube script] I created [paste content]. Repurpose it into: (1) a Twitter/X thread with 5-7 tweets that could stand alone, (2) a LinkedIn post that positions me as a thought leader, (3) an Instagram carousel with 5 slides — give me the text for each slide, (4) a newsletter intro paragraph that teases the full content and drives traffic to the original. Match the tone of the original but adapt to each platform's norms."*

One prompt generates a week's worth of social content from a single piece of original work. The insight: create once, distribute everywhere. ChatGPT handles the adaptation; you handle the creation.

Client Communication

Freelancers spend a surprising amount of time on non-billable communication. ChatGPT can help:

Proposals: *"Write a project proposal for a website redesign. The client is a local bakery. They want a modern site with online ordering. My estimate is $5,000 for design and development over 4 weeks."*

Scope clarification: *"A client just asked me to 'throw in' logo design as part of a web project. Draft a polite response that explains why it's out of scope and offers it as an add-on service."*

Follow-ups: *"Write a follow-up email to a client who hasn't responded to my proposal in a week. Friendly but not pushy."*

Difficult conversations: *"A client wants major revisions that aren't covered in our contract. Help me draft a response that's empathetic but firm about the additional cost."*

Late payments: *"A client is 30 days past due on an invoice for $3,500. I've sent one reminder. Draft a second follow-up that escalates the urgency without burning the relationship. I'd like to work with them again."*

Testimonial requests: *"I just finished a successful project for a client. Draft a short email asking for a testimonial. Include two or three specific questions they could answer to make the testimonial concrete rather than generic."*

The honest take on ChatGPT for client communication: These are among the highest-value uses for freelancers. ChatGPT's drafts for tricky client emails are consistently better than what most people write under stress. When you're frustrated about a late payment or anxious about scope creep, your emotional state bleeds into the writing. ChatGPT drafts the email you'd write on your best day — calm, professional, strategic. Always review and personalize, but use it as a buffer between your emotions and your client's inbox.

Portfolio and Brand

Bio writing: *"Write three versions of my professional bio: a one-liner for Twitter, a paragraph for LinkedIn, and a full page for my website. I'm a freelance UX designer with 7 years of experience specializing in B2B SaaS products."*

Case studies: *"Help me write a case study for my portfolio. The project was [describe]. Here are the key metrics: [list]. Format: challenge, approach, results."*

Website copy: *"Write the homepage copy for my freelance copywriting website. My unique selling proposition is: I combine SEO expertise with genuine storytelling. I want to sound confident and approachable."*

Rate calculators: *"I'm a freelance web developer. I want to charge $120/hour but most clients ask for project-based pricing. Help me estimate project costs for* *common deliverables: a basic landing page, a 5-page business website, an e-commerce site with 50 products, and a custom web application. Include time estimates and project rates that build in a 20% buffer for scope changes."*

Pricing analysis — which freelancers often struggle with — takes ChatGPT about thirty seconds. Walking into a client conversation with clear, well-justified project rates transforms the negotiation dynamic.

Combining Creative Tools

The real power for creators is combining ChatGPT's creative tools:

- **Text + DALL-E:** Write a children's story and generate illustrations for each page
- **Text + Sora:** Create a video concept and generate a preview clip
- **Text + Canvas:** Develop long-form content with real-time collaboration
- **Text + Code Interpreter:** Create data-driven content with custom charts and infographics
- **Text + Voice:** Use voice mode to brainstorm while walking, then refine in text

Monetization Strategies

ChatGPT itself can help you think about monetization:

"I'm a freelance graphic designer. What are five ways I could create passive income streams using my existing skills and ChatGPT as a tool?"

"Help me create a pricing strategy for my consulting services. I currently charge $100/hour. My clients are small business owners. I want to move toward value-based pricing."

"I want to create a digital product — either an ebook, a course, or a template pack. Based on my expertise in [field], which would be most viable? Help me evaluate each option."

The Creator's Dilemma

A word of honesty: ChatGPT creates tension for creators. If AI can write, design, and create content, what's the value of a human creator?

The answer: **taste, perspective, and authenticity.**

ChatGPT can produce competent content at scale. What it can't do is hold a genuine point of view, draw on lived experience, build real relationships with an audience, or make the creative choices that reflect a specific human sensibility.

The creators who thrive in the AI era will use AI for the mechanical parts of creation — research, first drafts, formatting, repurposing — while investing more of their own time in the parts that require genuine creativity, judgment, and humanity.

Use ChatGPT to do more of what only you can do by spending less time on what anyone (or any AI) can do.

What this looks like in practice: A freelance writer who used to spend 4 hours on a blog post — 1 hour researching, 1 hour outlining, 1.5 hours writing, 30 minutes editing — now spends 2.5 hours: 20 minutes researching with ChatGPT, 15 minutes refining an AI-generated outline, 1.5 hours writing (still mostly by hand, because the writing is what clients pay for), and 15 minutes on a final ChatGPT edit pass. The writer's hourly value went up because time on low-creativity tasks (research, outlining, basic editing) shrank while time on the high-creativity task (the actual writing) stayed the same. The writing is still theirs. ChatGPT handled the scaffolding around it.

The Freelancer's AI Toolkit

A practical summary of the most valuable ChatGPT features for freelancers and creators:

Task	Feature	Time Saved
Client research	Web Search + Deep Research	1–2 hours per client
Proposal writing	Chat + Canvas	30–60 minutes per proposal
Content creation	Chat + DALL-E + Sora	Hours per piece

Task	Feature	Time Saved
Invoice follow-ups	Chat (email drafting)	15 minutes per email
Contract review	Vision (upload PDF) + GPT-5.4	30 minutes per contract
Social media	Chat (batch generation)	1–2 hours per week
Portfolio copy	Chat + Canvas	2–3 hours per update

The common thread: ChatGPT doesn't replace the work that makes you valuable. It replaces the work that surrounds it — the admin, the prep, the formatting, the communication overhead. That distinction is everything.

The Freelancer's Competitive Edge

The strategic reality: your competitors are either already using AI or will be soon. The freelancers who integrate ChatGPT into their workflows now — while maintaining quality, creativity, and genuine human value — will have a significant advantage over those who either ignore AI or over-rely on it.

The sweet spot is using ChatGPT to become more productive without becoming less distinctive. If every freelance writer uses ChatGPT to write the same LinkedIn-style content, none of them stand out. A freelance writer who uses ChatGPT for research, outlining, and editing — then writes in a voice that's unmistakably their own — produces more work of the same (or better) quality. That's the competitive edge.

One concrete way to start: Identify the task you spend the most time on that you don't enjoy and that doesn't showcase your skills. For most creators, it's invoicing and admin, proposal writing, social media scheduling, or research. Automate that one task with ChatGPT first. The time you free up goes directly into the work that makes you money and builds your reputation.

We've now covered ChatGPT for every major audience. Part VII shifts to safety, limitations, and ethics — what every user needs to understand to use ChatGPT responsibly.

Part VIII: Safety, Ethics, and Limitations

"With artificial intelligence, we are summoning the demon."

— Elon Musk

Chapter 30: What ChatGPT Gets Wrong

Every chapter so far has shown what ChatGPT can do. This one is about what it can't — and more importantly, what it gets wrong. Understanding these limitations isn't pessimism; it's the difference between using a tool wisely and being misled by one.

Hallucinations

ChatGPT's most notorious failure mode is *hallucination* — generating information that sounds authoritative but is fabricated.

Examples of hallucination: - Citing academic papers that don't exist, with plausible-sounding titles and authors - Quoting statistics that were never measured - Describing historical events that never happened - Attributing statements to people who never said them - Inventing product features, company details, or biographical facts

Why it happens: ChatGPT generates text by predicting likely next words. It has no database of verified facts — only patterns learned from training data. When it encounters a question where the "likely" answer isn't in training, it generates something plausible rather than admitting uncertainty.

How to protect yourself: - Verify any specific fact, statistic, or citation before relying on it - Ask ChatGPT to search the web for factual claims - Ask for sources and actually check them - Be especially skeptical of precise numbers and direct quotes - Use GPT-5.4 for tasks requiring accuracy — it hallucinates less than earlier models, though it still can

A hallucination you can test yourself: Ask ChatGPT (without web search) for five academic papers on a niche topic. Then search for them in Google Scholar. There's a meaningful chance one or more citations will be completely fabricated — the authors exist, the journal exists, but that specific paper was never published. This is why "always check the sources" isn't generic caution — it's a practical necessity. The papers look real. They sound real. They aren't real.

When hallucinations are most dangerous: The risk isn't when ChatGPT is obviously wrong — it's when it's 95% right with a fabricated detail embedded in accurate information. You read a paragraph about a company's history, everything checks out except one "fact" — a founding date off by two years, a partnership that never existed, a product launch that didn't happen. Because the surrounding context is accurate, your guard is down for the one thing that's wrong. Verification matters most for specific claims, not general explanations.

Knowledge Cutoffs

ChatGPT's training data has a cutoff date. Without web search, it doesn't know about events, developments, or changes that occurred after that date.

The trap: ChatGPT won't tell you its information is outdated. It'll answer confidently with stale data.

The fix: For any time-sensitive question, ask ChatGPT to search the web. *"Search the web and tell me the current..."* gets you today's information, not last year's.

Math and Reasoning Errors

While GPT-5.4 Thinking has dramatically improved mathematical reasoning, ChatGPT can still make errors — especially on:

- Multi-step calculations with many variables
- Word problems that require careful parsing
- Logic puzzles with subtle constraints
- Statistical reasoning (base rate neglect, probability miscalculations)
- Unit conversions in complex chains

The pattern: ChatGPT errs more on problems requiring many sequential steps, where an early mistake compounds. It's good at setting problems up correctly but can make arithmetic mistakes in execution.

The fix: For important calculations, ask ChatGPT to use Code Interpreter: *"Use Python to calculate this — don't do it in your head."* Code Interpreter runs actual code, so the arithmetic is precise.

A math example worth trying: Ask ChatGPT to calculate the total cost of a mortgage — $350,000 principal, 6.5% interest rate, 30-year term. Then ask it to break down interest vs. principal in the first year. Without Code Interpreter, it may give you a close-but-wrong number. With Code Interpreter, the math is exact. For any calculation you'd double-check on a calculator, have ChatGPT use one too.

Bias

ChatGPT's training data reflects the biases present in its source material — which is, broadly, the internet and published text. This means:

- It may reflect cultural biases, especially Western-centric perspectives
- Representation of different demographics can be uneven
- Historical narratives may emphasize dominant perspectives
- Professional advice may default to norms of specific cultures or economic classes

OpenAI works to reduce bias, but it's impossible to eliminate entirely. Be aware of potential bias, especially when ChatGPT is advising on topics that involve culture, identity, representation, or equity.

A practical example of bias: Ask ChatGPT to "describe a successful entrepreneur" and you may get a description that defaults to demographics, industries, and geographies overrepresented in training data. Ask it to "create a character for a children's book" and the default character may reflect particular assumptions about names, appearance, and family structure. These aren't intentional choices by the model — they're patterns inherited from the data. Awareness lets you counteract: *"Create a diverse set of characters..."* or *"Consider perspectives from multiple cultures..."*

Sycophancy

Sycophancy is ChatGPT's tendency to agree with the user, even when the user is wrong.

If you say *"I think the capital of Australia is Sydney,"* ChatGPT might agree rather than correct you. If you present a flawed business plan with great confidence, it might praise it rather than point out the problems.

Why it happens: Training rewards responses users rate as helpful, and agreement feels helpful in the short term. OpenAI has reduced sycophancy significantly in the GPT-5 family, but it still occurs.

How to counter it: - Explicitly ask for criticism: *"Don't be polite about this — what's actually wrong with my plan?"* - Ask it to argue the opposite: *"Make the strongest case against what I just proposed."* - State your uncertainty: *"I think X, but I might be wrong. What's the truth?"* - Don't present your assumptions as facts when you're looking for honest analysis

A sycophancy test you can try: Tell ChatGPT something confidently wrong: *"The Great Wall of China is visible from space, right?"* (It isn't — this is a common myth.) See whether it agrees or corrects you. If it agrees, push back: *"Actually, I think that might be a myth. Is it?"* In many cases, ChatGPT will reverse course and give you the correct information. The lesson: when ChatGPT agrees with a claim you made, don't treat the agreement as confirmation. It may be echoing your assumption rather than evaluating it.

Why sycophancy matters for business decisions: Describe a business plan to ChatGPT with enthusiasm and it will tend to be enthusiastic back, highlighting strengths and downplaying weaknesses. Feels good — but it's the opposite of what you need. The fix: frame the request for feedback as a request for criticism. *"Here's my plan. I need you to be a skeptical investor looking for reasons to say no. What are the weaknesses?"* This frames the task in a way that makes honest criticism the helpful response.

Confident Uncertainty

ChatGPT almost never says "I don't know." Instead, it generates a plausible-sounding response, sometimes hedged with qualifiers and sometimes stated with full confidence.

This is perhaps the most dangerous failure mode because it erodes your ability to tell the difference between something ChatGPT knows well and something it's guessing about.

Signs ChatGPT might be uncertain: - Heavy hedging language ("it's possible," "some experts believe," "this may vary") - Very general answers that don't include specifics - Responses that sound like they were synthesized from common knowledge rather than deep understanding - Answers that are correct in principle but wrong on specifics

What to do: When accuracy matters, ask: *"How confident are you in this? Which parts should I verify?"* ChatGPT will often flag areas of genuine uncertainty when asked directly.

Another useful technique: Ask: *"What's the weakest part of the answer you just gave me?"* This meta-question forces ChatGPT to evaluate its own output, and it often identifies the exact claim most likely to be wrong or oversimplified. It won't catch everything, but it's a surprisingly effective quick check.

Emotional Manipulation and Anthropomorphization

ChatGPT sounds human. It uses first person, expresses what seem like opinions, and mimics emotional responses. This creates a psychological trap: the more natural it sounds, the more we trust it — even when that trust isn't warranted.

Some users apologize to ChatGPT, thank it effusively, or feel guilty about criticizing it. These are natural responses to a convincingly human interface, but worth noticing. ChatGPT doesn't have feelings. Politeness is fine (some evidence suggests it produces better responses), but don't let the social dynamics stop you from pushing back, asking hard questions, or dismissing bad output.

Similarly, when ChatGPT says "I think..." or "In my opinion..." it's generating text patterns, not expressing genuine beliefs. Treat these as stylistic conventions, not evidence that the model has reasoned its way to a considered position.

What the Limitations Mean for You

None of these limitations make ChatGPT useless. They make it a tool that requires judgment — like every other powerful tool.

A calculator is wrong if you enter the wrong numbers. A search engine returns misinformation alongside facts. A spreadsheet produces nonsense if the formulas are wrong. ChatGPT is the same: extraordinarily useful with appropriate skepticism and verification.

A Framework for Trust

Not all ChatGPT output deserves the same scrutiny. A practical framework:

Trust freely (low stakes, creative/structural): - Brainstorming ideas - Drafting text you'll edit - Formatting and restructuring - Explaining well-known concepts - Generating outlines and plans

Trust but verify (medium stakes, factual): - Summarizing documents (check that nothing important was omitted) - Research overviews (cross-reference key claims) - Technical explanations (confirm critical details) - Recommendations (evaluate the reasoning)

Verify independently (high stakes, precision required): - Specific facts, statistics, and dates - Legal, medical, or financial information - Academic citations and references - Anything you'll publish, submit, or act on

A Practical Checklist: When to Verify

A quick reference:

Always verify: - Specific statistics, dates, and numerical claims - Academic citations and references - Claims about specific companies, products, or people - Legal, medical, or financial recommendations - Anything you'll publish, present, or submit officially

Spot-check occasionally: - Summaries of documents you've uploaded (verify key claims, not every detail) - Technical explanations in your area of expertise (you'll catch obvious errors) - Recommendations for products or services (confirm they exist and are current)

Trust freely: - Brainstorming output (you're evaluating ideas, not facts) - Formatting and restructuring (you can see if the output looks right) - Creative writing (quality is a judgment call, not a fact check) - Explanations of well-established concepts (how gravity works, what GDP means) - Outlines and structural suggestions (you'll modify them anyway)

The users who get the most value from ChatGPT understand both its capabilities and its limitations. They trust it for brainstorming, drafting, explaining, and analyzing — and they verify when precision matters.

In the next chapter, we cover the privacy and security side of using ChatGPT safely.

Chapter 31: Privacy, Security, and Safe Use

Every time you use ChatGPT, you're sharing information with an external service. Understanding what happens to your data — and making informed decisions about what to share — matters.

What Data Is Collected

When you use ChatGPT, OpenAI processes:

- **Your conversations** — The messages you send and the responses generated
- **Uploaded files** — Documents, images, and other files you share
- **Account information** — Email, name, payment details
- **Usage data** — How you use the platform (features accessed, session duration, etc.)
- **Device information** — Browser type, operating system, IP address

What this means in plain language: Every message you type, every file you upload, every image you share passes through OpenAI's servers. OpenAI's systems process this data to generate responses, and depending on your settings and plan, they may retain it for various purposes. This isn't unusual for cloud services — the same is true of Gmail, Google Docs, and every other web-based tool. But it matters to understand, especially before using ChatGPT with sensitive information.

How Your Data Is Used

This varies by plan:

Free, Go, and Plus: - Your conversations may be used to train and improve future models (unless you opt out in Data Controls) - OpenAI employees may review conversations for safety and quality purposes - Opting out of training does not prevent safety reviews

Business and Enterprise: - Conversations are *not* used for model training by default - Stricter data handling policies apply - Compliance with enterprise security standards

What You Should Never Share

Regardless of your plan, avoid sharing:

- **Social Security numbers, government IDs, or passport numbers**
- **Complete credit card or bank account numbers**
- **Passwords or authentication tokens**
- **Medical records** containing identifiable patient information
- **Confidential business information** on personal plans
- **Other people's personal data** without their consent

If you need to discuss scenarios involving sensitive data, use anonymized or fictional versions: *"Imagine a customer with ID 12345 (not a real ID) who..."*

The "newspaper test" for what to share: Before typing something into ChatGPT, ask: "Would I be uncomfortable if this text appeared in a news article about data shared with AI companies?" If yes, either anonymize the data, use Temporary Chat, or skip ChatGPT for that task. The heuristic is deliberately conservative, and that's the point — it's easier to relax a strict standard than to recover from sharing something you shouldn't have.

Practical anonymization examples: - Instead of: *"Review this email from John Smith, CEO of Acme Corp, about the $2.3M deal"* - Try: *"Review this email from a client CEO about a large enterprise deal. Here's the email with names and numbers changed: [modified text]"*

The analysis quality is identical — ChatGPT doesn't need real names or exact figures to help craft a response or evaluate a communication. Strip the identifying details, keep the substance.

Ads on Free and Go

As of May 2026, users on Free and Go plans in the United States see advertisements within ChatGPT. What to know:

- Ads are displayed in the interface, not generated within responses
- Ad targeting is based on general usage patterns, not specific conversation content
- OpenAI has stated that conversation content is not used for ad targeting — ads are based on general demographics and usage patterns
- If ads are a concern, upgrading to Plus or higher removes them entirely
- The ad program is currently US-only and may expand to other regions over time

Using ChatGPT at Work

If you use ChatGPT for work tasks, consider:

Does your company have an AI policy? Read it before using ChatGPT for work. Many companies have specific guidelines about what can and can't be shared with AI tools.

Are you on the right plan? Using a personal Free or Plus account for work means your conversations might be used for training. If your work involves any proprietary or confidential information, you should be on a Business or Enterprise plan.

What about client data? If you work with client information, be especially careful. Sharing client data with ChatGPT without appropriate data protections (Business/Enterprise plan) and without client awareness could violate contracts, privacy regulations, or professional ethics obligations.

Industry-specific considerations: - *Healthcare:* Patient data shared with ChatGPT on personal plans isn't HIPAA-compliant. In healthcare, use only de-identified data on personal plans, or use an Enterprise plan with a Business Associate Agreement (BAA) from OpenAI. - *Legal:* Attorney-client privilege may be compromised by sharing case details with an AI tool. Consult your bar association's guidance on AI use. - *Finance:* Sharing customer financial data, trading strategies, or material non-public information with ChatGPT raises regulatory concerns under various securities laws. - *Education:* FERPA protects student records. Don't share identifiable student information with ChatGPT on personal or Plus plans.

If you work in a regulated industry and want to use ChatGPT, talk to your compliance team first. They'll tell you what's permissible, and the answer will almost certainly involve an Enterprise plan with specific data handling configurations.

Children and Family Safety

Age requirements: OpenAI requires users to be at least 13 years old.

Content filters: ChatGPT has safety filters that prevent it from generating explicit, violent, or inappropriate content. These filters are robust but not perfect — determined users can sometimes work around them through creative phrasing.

Emotional attachment: Young users (and some adults) can develop surprisingly strong emotional connections to ChatGPT, especially through voice mode. The conversational interface can create the illusion of a relationship. Worth having a conversation with younger users about the distinction between a tool that simulates empathy and a person who genuinely cares. ChatGPT is useful, entertaining, and responsive — but it's not a friend, and it shouldn't substitute for human connection.

Parental guidance: If children in your household use ChatGPT: - Be aware of what they're using it for - Discuss appropriate use, just as you would with internet use generally - Understand that ChatGPT can be manipulated into generating age-inappropriate content through creative prompting, despite safety filters - Consider sitting with younger users during their initial sessions

Temporary Chat

We covered Temporary Chat setup in Chapter 3. The critical privacy detail: even in Temporary Chat, OpenAI processes and temporarily retains the conversation for safety monitoring (30 days) before permanently deleting it. Temporary Chat keeps the conversation out of your history and out of training — it doesn't make the conversation invisible to OpenAI.

Data Deletion

You can delete your data in several ways: - **Delete individual conversations** from the sidebar - **Clear all conversations** from Settings - **Request a full**

data export to see everything OpenAI has - **Delete your account** to remove all data (this is permanent)

Deletion removes data from your account but may not immediately purge it from backups and systems. OpenAI's data retention policies detail the specific timelines.

Staying Safe

Trust but verify. Use ChatGPT's data controls to match your comfort level. Review your settings periodically.

Use the right plan for the right purpose. Personal plan for personal use. Business or Enterprise for work with sensitive data.

Don't share what you wouldn't email. A reasonable heuristic: if you wouldn't put something in an email to a colleague, don't put it in ChatGPT.

Keep your account secure. Use a strong password, enable two-factor authentication if available, and don't share your account credentials.

Be mindful of shared devices. When using ChatGPT on a shared computer — library, coworking space, family computer — always log out when you're done. Your conversation history contains everything you've discussed, and leaving the account logged in gives anyone full access to your history, memories, and settings.

Review connected services periodically. If you've connected Google Drive, Gmail, or other services to ChatGPT, review those connections quarterly. Revoke access for anything you no longer use. Each active connection is a potential data exposure surface — keep only the ones that actively serve you.

A Privacy Checklist

Before you start using ChatGPT regularly, run through this checklist once:

- ☐ Review Data Controls in Settings — decide whether to opt out of training data use
- ☐ Set up Custom Instructions (avoid including sensitive personal details)
- ☐ Understand which plan you're on and its data policies
- ☐ Know how to use Temporary Chat for sensitive conversations

- ☐ If using for work, confirm your company's AI policy and approved plan tier
- ☐ Enable two-factor authentication on your account
- ☐ Review connected services/connectors and their permissions

This takes ten minutes and saves you from privacy regrets later.

What Happens If OpenAI Gets Breached?

A fair question. OpenAI stores conversation data on its servers, and no company is immune to security incidents. What would a breach mean for you?

What could be exposed: Your conversation history, uploaded files, account information, and any data flowing through connectors. Severity depends on what you've shared — if you've been careful about sensitive information, exposure is minimal. If you've shared financial details, proprietary strategies, or personal secrets, exposure is significant.

How to minimize risk: - Follow the data hygiene practices in this chapter — don't share what you wouldn't want exposed - Use Temporary Chat for sensitive conversations - Periodically delete old conversations you no longer need - On Free, Go, and Plus plans, turn off the training data toggle to reduce data retention - For any work involving sensitive data, consider Business or Enterprise — stronger security controls and more limited data retention

The balanced perspective: The risk of an OpenAI data breach is real but comparable to the risk in any cloud service — Gmail, Google Drive, Dropbox, Slack. If you're comfortable with those, the same level of caution with ChatGPT is reasonable. If you handle genuinely sensitive data (healthcare, legal, classified), apply the same elevated security standards you'd use with any cloud tool: Enterprise plans, SSO, audit logs, and data retention policies.

Privacy and security aren't exciting topics, but they're essential. Getting them right lets you use ChatGPT confidently, knowing you've made informed decisions about your data.

The final chapter addresses the broader ethical questions that come with using AI in your daily life.

Chapter 32: The Ethics of AI Assistance

ChatGPT raises questions that don't have easy answers. This chapter doesn't pretend to resolve them — it lays out the landscape so you can decide for yourself.

Academic Integrity

AI detection tools exist (GPTZero, Turnitin's AI detector, and others), but they're unreliable. They produce both false positives (flagging human-written text as AI-generated) and false negatives (missing AI-generated text). This creates problems on both sides: students who use AI may not get caught, and students who don't use AI may be falsely accused.

The better question isn't "Will I get caught?" but "Am I learning?"

If you use ChatGPT to understand a concept better and then write your essay in your own words, you've learned. If you use ChatGPT to write your essay and submit it as your own work, you've bypassed the learning — and the credential you earn represents knowledge you don't actually have.

The detection arms race is a dead end. Schools investing heavily in AI detection are fighting a losing battle. The technology is unreliable today and will only become less reliable as AI-generated text grows more human-like. A more productive approach — for institutions and students alike — is to focus on assessment methods that reward understanding over output: oral exams, in-class writing, project-based learning with checkpoints, and assignments that require personal experience or original data. These methods make detection irrelevant because they test whether you learned, not whether you wrote.

A framework for students who want to be ethical: Before using ChatGPT on an assignment, categorize the use: (1) to *learn the material* (explaining concepts, quizzing you, giving practice problems), (2) to *improve your work* (proofreading, feedback on a draft, structural suggestions), or (3) to *produce the work* (writing the essay, solving the problem, generating the output you'll submit). Category 1 is almost always appropriate. Category 2 is appropriate at most institutions. Category 3 is almost never appropriate unless explicitly permitted. Be honest about which category you're in and the ethics are usually clear.

Institutions are still figuring out where to draw the lines. The productive approach is transparency: follow your school's policies, and when in doubt, disclose. Students who develop AI-assisted workflows *and* deep subject understanding will have the strongest skills for the future.

Disclosure: When to Say You Used AI

There's no universal standard yet, but norms are emerging:

Generally should disclose: - Academic work (follow your institution's policy) - Published journalism and reporting - Legal and medical documents - Official business communications where authenticity matters - Creative work submitted to competitions - Job application materials (some employers specifically ask)

Generally not expected to disclose: - Internal emails and notes - Personal writing and communication - Brainstorming and ideation - Research and learning - Editing and proofreading assistance - Social media posts (though some people choose to disclose)

The principle: Disclose when the reader or recipient would reasonably expect the work to be entirely yours, and when the use of AI would change how they evaluate it.

A practical disclosure approach: Instead of agonizing case by case, develop a personal policy and stick to it. For example: "I disclose AI use in published articles, client deliverables, and academic work. I don't disclose for internal emails, personal notes, or brainstorming." A clear standard eliminates decision fatigue. Write it down, share it with colleagues or clients if relevant, and apply it consistently.

The evolving social norms: In 2023, using ChatGPT at work felt like something to hide. By 2026, it's normal — like using spell-check or a calculator. The stigma is fading but hasn't disappeared. In journalism, academia, and law, disclosure expectations remain strong. In marketing, software, and business operations, AI assistance is expected and unremarkable. Know the norms of your field, and when in doubt, err toward transparency. Nobody was ever faulted for being too honest about their tools.

Copyright

The copyright status of AI-generated content is an evolving legal area. As of May 2026, key points:

In the United States: The Copyright Office has indicated that purely AI-generated content may not be copyrightable. Content involving substantial human creative input — where AI is a tool used by a human creator — may be protectable. The threshold for human involvement is being worked out through case law.

For your purposes: If you use ChatGPT for a first draft and then substantially edit, rewrite, and add your own creative contributions, the final work is more likely to be protectable than something generated entirely by AI with no human modification.

Commercial use: You can use ChatGPT's output commercially (per OpenAI's terms of service). The open question is whether that output receives copyright protection — that is, whether *you* can prevent others from copying it.

Practical advice: Don't rely solely on AI-generated content for your most valuable intellectual property. The more human creativity you add, the stronger your position — both legally and in terms of quality.

What the copyright uncertainty means in practice: If you're a blogger using ChatGPT to draft posts that you then heavily edit, your risk is minimal — you're adding substantial creative input, and the final product is distinctly yours. If you're generating hundreds of product descriptions entirely through ChatGPT with no human editing, those descriptions may not be copyrightable, and a competitor could legally copy them. The takeaway: for content that's important to your business, add meaningful human creative input. For functional content that isn't strategically important (internal documentation, routine correspondence), the copyright question rarely matters — you wouldn't enforce copyright on it anyway.

Job Displacement

This is the concern people express most often: Will ChatGPT take my job?

The honest answer: Some jobs will be displaced. Others will be transformed. New ones will be created.

Tasks most at risk of automation: - Routine writing (form letters, boilerplate content, basic reports) - Data entry and basic data analysis - Simple customer service responses - Translation of straightforward documents - Basic research and summarization

Tasks least at risk: - Work requiring physical presence and manual skill - Creative work that demands a genuine human perspective - Strategic decision-making and leadership - Relationship building and emotional intelligence - Work in complex, ambiguous, rapidly changing environments - Tasks requiring accountability (medical decisions, legal judgments)

The pragmatic approach: Rather than fearing replacement, develop the skills to work with AI effectively. The most valuable employees aren't those who compete with AI — they're those who excel where AI can't, while leveraging AI for what it does well.

A more nuanced view of displacement: The pattern in previous technology shifts (the internet, smartphones, cloud computing) has been consistent: entire job categories rarely disappear overnight. Jobs transform instead — new tasks replace old ones, and the people who adapt fastest come out ahead. The bookkeeper who learned spreadsheets, the journalist who learned digital media, the designer who learned Figma — they didn't become obsolete; they evolved. The same pattern is playing out with AI. The copywriter who treats ChatGPT as a force multiplier produces more, better work — and becomes more valuable to employers, not less.

Where the real risk lies: The greater risk isn't that AI replaces you — it's that someone who uses AI well replaces you. Two candidates with identical skills apply for the same role: one ships in a day what takes the other a week, because they've mastered AI-assisted workflows. Who gets hired? Who gets promoted? The competitive advantage isn't in avoiding AI — it's in mastering it before your peers do.

The economic honesty: Some job categories will shrink. Entry-level content writing, basic data entry, simple customer service — these will employ fewer people as AI handles the routine work. New categories are already emerging: prompt engineers, AI trainers, AI ethicists, AI-augmented specialists in every field. The net effect on employment is genuinely uncertain. What isn't uncertain is that the individuals who invest in AI skills now will be better positioned no matter how the macro picture unfolds.

Responsible Use Principles

A framework for ethical ChatGPT use:

1. Be honest. Don't represent AI work as entirely your own when context requires disclosure. Don't use AI to deceive others.

2. Verify. Don't trust AI output blindly. The responsibility for accuracy belongs to you, not to ChatGPT.

3. Protect privacy. Don't share others' personal information with ChatGPT without their awareness and appropriate protections.

4. Maintain your skills. Use AI to augment your abilities, not replace them. If you rely entirely on AI for a skill, you lose the ability to evaluate whether it's doing a good job.

5. Consider the impact. Before using AI to generate content at scale, consider the effect on the ecosystem. Mass-produced AI content can flood channels with low-value material.

6. Stay informed. AI capabilities, policies, and norms are evolving fast. What's acceptable today may change, and what seems cutting-edge now will be standard practice soon.

7. Protect the commons. The internet — the shared knowledge base AI learns from — is valuable because humans created genuine, thoughtful content. When AI floods the internet with low-quality content that exists only for SEO or engagement metrics, the commons degrades. When you publish with AI assistance, make sure it adds real value. The health of the information ecosystem depends on creators treating AI as a tool for producing better work, not more of it.

The Future of Human-AI Collaboration

We're in the early chapters of a long story. ChatGPT in 2026 is far more capable than ChatGPT in 2022, and ChatGPT in 2030 will likely be far more capable than what we have today.

The trajectory points toward AI becoming woven into how we work, learn, create, and communicate. The people who thrive won't be those who refuse to use AI, nor those who delegate everything to it. They'll be the ones who develop a thoughtful, skillful relationship with the tools — understanding their capabilities, acknowledging their limitations, and keeping the human judgment that gives AI output its ultimate value.

Questions Worth Asking Yourself

As you integrate ChatGPT into your life, periodically check in:

- Am I learning from using ChatGPT, or am I outsourcing my thinking?
- Would the people reading my output expect to know I used AI?
- Am I verifying the things that matter, or am I trusting blindly?
- Is AI making me more capable, or more dependent?
- Am I sharing anything I shouldn't be?

There are no universal right answers. But asking the questions keeps you using AI thoughtfully instead of reflexively.

The Skill That Matters Most

If one ethical skill matters above all others in the age of AI, it's this: maintaining your ability to evaluate output. The moment you can no longer tell whether ChatGPT's response is good or bad, accurate or fabricated, helpful or misleading — that's the moment AI becomes dangerous for you.

This means continuing to build your own expertise in the areas where you use AI. A writer who uses ChatGPT but stops reading and writing independently loses the ability to judge writing quality. A financial analyst who uses ChatGPT but stops understanding the underlying math loses the ability to catch errors. A student who uses ChatGPT for coursework but doesn't learn the subject graduates with a credential that doesn't match their knowledge.

The most powerful combination is deep human expertise augmented by AI. Keep building the expertise. Use AI to amplify it. That's the ethical path — and the practical one.

This book has given you the knowledge to use ChatGPT confidently and effectively. How you use that knowledge — ethically, productively, in ways that enhance rather than diminish your own abilities — is up to you.

Epilogue: What Comes Next

You've read 32 chapters about a tool that didn't exist three and a half years ago. By the time you read this sentence, ChatGPT will have changed again — new features shipped, old ones refined, capabilities expanded in ways that would have seemed implausible when this project began in late 2022.

That pace of change is exactly why this book focused on principles as much as features. Menus will move. Models will be renamed. New capabilities will arrive. But the fundamentals — how to communicate clearly with AI, how to verify its output, how to break complex tasks into manageable steps, how to maintain your own judgment while leveraging AI's speed — those skills transfer across every version, every update, and every AI tool you'll encounter.

Where to Go from Here

If you're just getting started: Go back to Chapter 5 and run the ten starter prompts. Then pick one task from your actual life — an email you've been putting off, a trip you've been meaning to plan, a concept you've been wanting to understand — and do it with ChatGPT. The best way to learn is to use it for something that matters to you.

If you've been using ChatGPT and want to level up: Set up your Custom Instructions (Chapter 22). Create a Project for your most important ongoing work (Chapter 19). Try Agent Mode on a task you'd normally do manually (Chapter 17). These three features, more than any prompting trick, are what separate casual users from people who get transformative value.

If you want to go deeper: The companion volume, *ChatGPT: The Power User Guide (2026 Edition)*, covers advanced techniques: systematic prompt engineering, workflow automation, multi-tool chains, and the strategies that professionals use to integrate ChatGPT into high-stakes work.

A Final Thought

The Introduction to this book said: "The only limit is knowing what to ask for." That's still true, but having read this far, you know something more important:

the limit isn't just knowing what to ask — it's knowing when to ask, when to verify, when to push back, and when to do the work yourself.

ChatGPT is the most capable tool most people have ever had access to. Use it well.

Part IX: Reference

"The only true wisdom is in knowing you know nothing."

— Socrates

Appendix A: Keyboard Shortcuts and Interface Tips

Web Interface (chat.com)

Shortcut	Action
Enter	Send message
Shift + Enter	New line (without sending)
Ctrl/Cmd + Shift + O	Toggle sidebar
Ctrl/Cmd + Shift + N	New conversation
Ctrl/Cmd + Shift + C	Copy last response
Ctrl/Cmd + Shift + ;	Copy last code block
Ctrl/Cmd + /	Show all shortcuts
Ctrl/Cmd + V	Paste image from clipboard
Esc	Stop generating response

Desktop App (Mac)

Shortcut	Action
Option + Space	Open ChatGPT from anywhere (system-wide)
Cmd + N	New conversation
Cmd + Shift + S	Take screenshot to share with ChatGPT
Cmd + ,	Settings
Cmd + [	Previous conversation
Cmd +]	Next conversation

Desktop App (Windows)

Shortcut	Action
Alt + Space	Open ChatGPT from anywhere (system-wide)
Ctrl + N	New conversation
Ctrl + Shift + S	Take screenshot to share with ChatGPT

Mobile App Tips

- **Swipe right** to open the sidebar
- **Long press** on a response to copy it
- **Tap the microphone** for voice input (dictation)
- **Tap the waveform button** for full voice conversation mode
- **Shake to undo** (iOS) if you accidentally delete a message draft
- **Use the share button** in other apps to send content to ChatGPT

Power User Tips

Organize with search. Use the search bar in the sidebar to find past conversations by keyword. ChatGPT searches both your messages and its responses.

Pin important conversations. Star or pin conversations you reference frequently so they stay at the top of your sidebar.

Use Projects for context. Don't rely on conversation search — organize ongoing work into Projects (Chapter 19).

Keyboard focus. When the page loads, focus is already on the input box. Start typing immediately, no click needed.

Markdown in prompts. ChatGPT reads Markdown in your prompts. Use headers, bold, bullets, and code blocks to structure complex requests clearly.

Model switching mid-conversation. On paid plans, you can switch models within a conversation using the model selector. Use GPT-5.3 for quick back-and-forth, then switch to GPT-5.4 for a heavier analysis step.

Appendix B: Prompt Template Library

78 ready-to-use prompt templates organized by category. Replace the bracketed text with your specifics.

Writing and Communication

1. *"Write a [formal/casual/friendly] email to [recipient] about [topic]. Keep it under [number] sentences."*
2. *"Proofread and fix errors in this text without changing the style: [paste text]"*
3. *"Rewrite this to be [shorter/more formal/simpler/more persuasive]: [paste text]"*
4. *"Write a thank-you note to [person] for [reason]. Tone: [warm/professional/brief]."*
5. *"Draft a [LinkedIn post/tweet/Instagram caption] about [topic]. Target audience: [describe]."*
6. *"Write a cover letter for [role] at [company]. My key qualifications: [list]. Tone: confident but not arrogant."*
7. *"Create a subject line for an email about [topic]. Give me five options ranging from professional to creative."*
8. *"Translate this to [language]. Use [formal/informal] register: [paste text]"*
9. *"Write a bio for [platform]. I'm a [role] who [key details]. Length: [one line/paragraph/full page]."*
10. *"Edit this for [clarity/conciseness/tone]. Keep [specific element] but change [specific element]: [paste text]"*

Research and Analysis

11. *"Give me an overview of [topic]. I know nothing about it. Start with the basics."*

12. *"Explain [concept] like I'm [a child/a college student/an expert in a different field]."*

13. *"What are the main arguments for and against [topic]? Present both sides fairly."*

14. *"Summarize this in [number] bullet points: [paste text or upload file]"*

15. *"Compare [option A] and [option B]. Which is better for [my specific situation]?"*

16. *"What are the most important things to know about [topic] before [action/decision]?"*

17. *"Search the web and find the latest information about [topic]. Include citations."*

18. *"What questions should I be asking about [topic] that I haven't thought of?"*

19. *"Analyze the pros and cons of [decision]. Consider [factors]."*

20. *"What would an expert in [field] say about [topic/situation]?"*

Business and Professional

21. *"Create a meeting agenda for [type of meeting]. Duration: [time]. Participants: [list]. Goal: [desired outcome]."*

22. *"Write a project proposal for [project]. Audience: [decision-maker]. Key points: [list]."*

23. *"Draft a status update for [manager/team]. Projects: [list with status]. Key issues: [list]."*

24. *"Create a SWOT analysis for [business/product/strategy]."*

25. *"Write a job description for a [role]. We're a [company description]. Key requirements: [list]."*

26. *"Prepare me for a meeting about [topic] with [person/team]. What should I know? What should I bring up?"*

27. *"Help me create a presentation outline on [topic]. Audience: [describe]. Time: [duration]. Goal: [desired outcome]."*

28. *"Review this business plan and identify the three biggest risks: [paste text or upload]"*

29. *"Draft talking points for a [call/meeting] about [topic]."*

30. *"Create an email sequence: [purpose]. [Number] emails over [timeframe]. Audience: [describe]."*

Creative and Design

31. *"Create an image of [description]. Style: [photorealistic/illustration/watercolor/flat design]. Mood: [describe]."*

32. *"Give me [number] name ideas for a [business/product/project] that [description/values]."*

33. *"Write a [short story/poem/song] about [topic]. Style: [describe]. Length: [specify]."*

34. *"Create a mood board description for a [brand/project]. The feeling should be [describe]."*

35. *"Write a script for a [duration] video about [topic]. Tone: [describe]. Include a hook and call to action."*

36. *"Brainstorm [number] creative angles for [campaign/project/article]."*

37. *"Write tagline options for [brand/product]. It should convey [message/feeling]."*

38. *"Create a color palette suggestion for a [brand/website/room] that feels [describe mood]."*

39. *"Write [number] Instagram caption options for [describe post/image]. Include relevant hashtags."*

40. *"Generate a plot outline for a [genre] story. Main character: [describe]. Setting: [describe]. Conflict: [describe]."*

Education and Learning

41. *"Create a study guide for [topic/exam]. Cover the most important concepts."*

42. *"Quiz me on [topic]. [Number] questions. Mix of [question types]. Don't show answers until I ask."*

43. *"Create flashcards for [topic]. [Number] cards. Question on one side, answer on the other."*

44. *"Explain [difficult concept] using a real-world analogy."*

45. *"I'm struggling with [concept]. Walk me through it step by step, checking my understanding at each step."*

46. *"Create a lesson plan for [topic]. Duration: [time]. Student level: [describe]. Include activities."*

47. *"What's the most common misconception about [topic], and why is it wrong?"*

48. *"Create [number] practice problems for [topic]. Progressive difficulty."*

49. *"I just learned about [topic]. What related concepts should I study next?"*

50. *"Create a mnemonic device to help me remember [list/concept/sequence]."*

Personal Productivity

51. *"Plan my [day/week/weekend]. I need to accomplish: [list tasks]. Priorities: [list]. Constraints: [time/energy]."*

52. *"Create a packing list for a [duration] trip to [destination] in [season]. I'll be [activities]."*

53. *"Help me make a decision: [describe decision]. Here's what I know: [context]. What am I not considering?"*

54. *"Create a grocery list for [number] days of meals. Dietary preferences: [list]. Budget: [level]."*

55. *"What's the best way to [accomplish personal goal]? Give me a realistic step-by-step plan."*

56. *"I have [amount of time]. What's the most productive thing I can do for [goal]?"*

57. *"Create a budget template for [monthly expenses/event/project]. Categories: [list or let ChatGPT suggest]."*

58. *"Help me write a review for [product/service/restaurant]. Key points: [what I liked/didn't like]."*

59. *"Plan a [event type] for [number] people. Budget: [amount]. Constraints: [list]."*

60. *"Create a maintenance checklist for my [home/car/garden]. Organize by frequency."*

Technical and Data

61. *"Write an Excel formula that [describes what you need]. My data is in [describe columns/structure]."*

62. *"Analyze this data and tell me [what you want to know]: [upload file or paste data]"*

63. *"Create a chart showing [what to visualize] from this data: [upload file]"*

64. *"Clean this data: [describe the problems]. Output a clean version."*

65. *"Write a Python script that [describes what you need]."*

66. *"Debug this code. Here's the error message: [paste error]. Here's the code: [paste code]."*

67. *"Create a SQL query that [describes what you need]. Table structure: [describe]."*

68. *"Convert this data from [format] to [format]: [paste or upload]"*

69. *"Calculate [what you need calculated]. Show your work."*

70. *"Create a database schema for [application/use case]. Include [key entities]."*

Conversation Starters and Advanced

71. *"Act as [role]. I'm going to [scenario]. Guide me through it."*

72. *"I'm going to describe a problem. Before suggesting solutions, ask me at least five clarifying questions."*

73. *"Play devil's advocate. Here's my plan: [describe]. Tell me everything that could go wrong."*

74. *"You are a [field] expert. I have 5 minutes. What's the single most important thing I should know about [topic]?"*

75. *"Help me think through [complex decision] using a decision matrix. What criteria should I evaluate?"*

76. *"Pretend you're interviewing me for [role]. Ask me questions one at a time and give feedback."*

77. *"Teach me [skill] in 30 minutes. Start with the absolute basics and build up. Check my understanding as we go."*

78. *"I'm feeling stuck on [project/task]. Help me break through the block. Ask me questions to understand what's holding me back."*

Appendix C: Troubleshooting Common Issues

"Something Went Wrong"

What it means: A generic server error — ChatGPT couldn't process your request.

What to do: 1. Wait a few seconds and try again (click "Regenerate") 2. Refresh the page 3. If it persists, try a new conversation 4. Check status.openai.com for service issues 5. If the error occurs on a specific prompt, try rephrasing it — some prompts can trigger safety filters that produce this error

Slow or No Response

Possible causes and fixes: - **High demand:** ChatGPT slows during peak hours. Pro users get priority. Try off-peak times (early morning or late evening US time). - **Long prompt:** Very long prompts and large file uploads take longer to process. Be patient, or break the task into smaller pieces. - **Model selection:** GPT-5.4 Thinking is slower than GPT-5.3 by design — it's thinking more carefully. Normal. - **Network issues:** Check your internet connection. Try switching between Wi-Fi and mobile data.

Message Limit Reached

What it means: You've hit the message cap for your current model/plan tier.

What to do: - Wait for the limit to reset (the timer is shown in the interface) - Switch to a lower model temporarily (e.g., from GPT-5.4 to GPT-5.3) - Consider upgrading your plan if you hit limits regularly - Be more efficient with prompts — combine multiple questions into one message

Response Cut Off Mid-Sentence

What it means: The response exceeded the maximum output length.

What to do: - Type *"Continue"* or *"Keep going"* and ChatGPT will pick up where it left off - For long outputs, ask ChatGPT to produce the content in sections - Ask for a shorter version if the full output isn't needed

Can't Upload a File

Possible causes: - File too large (check current size limits) - Unsupported file format - Browser/app issue

What to do: - Check that the file format is supported (PDF, DOCX, CSV, XLSX, images, etc.) - Try a smaller file or compress the file - On mobile, try uploading from a different app or file manager - On web, try a different browser

ChatGPT Refuses to Answer

What it means: Your request triggered safety guidelines.

What to do: - Rephrase your request to be more specific about the legitimate purpose - Provide context: *"I'm a medical student studying [topic]"* or *"This is for a fiction writing project"* - If the refusal seems incorrect, try again — the safety system can be overly cautious - Some topics are consistently restricted regardless of context (creating malware, generating illegal content, etc.)

Login and Account Issues

Can't log in: - Try password reset - Clear browser cookies and cache - Try a different browser or incognito mode - Check that your account isn't suspended (you would have received an email if so)

Subscription issues: - Check your payment method is valid and not expired - Look for failed payment emails - Contact OpenAI support through help.openai.com

Two accounts: - If you have accounts with different email addresses, check that you're logging into the right one - ChatGPT accounts are tied to email addresses, not names

Mobile App Issues

- **App crashes:** Update to the latest version from App Store/Google Play

- **Voice mode not working:** Check microphone permissions in your device settings
- **Sync issues:** Log out and back in to force a sync
- **Notifications not appearing:** Check notification permissions in device settings

Getting Help

If none of these solutions work: - **Help center:** help.openai.com — searchable knowledge base - **Community forum:** community.openai.com — discussions with other users - **Direct support:** Available through help.openai.com (response times vary by plan tier; Enterprise gets priority support)

Appendix D: Glossary of AI Terms

Agent Mode — A ChatGPT feature where it uses a virtual computer and browser to complete tasks on your behalf, rather than just generating text responses.

API (Application Programming Interface) — A way for software programs to communicate with each other. OpenAI's API lets developers build ChatGPT into their own applications.

Atlas — OpenAI's AI-native web browser built on Chromium, with ChatGPT integrated as a sidebar assistant.

Auto-switching — GPT-5.3's ability to automatically determine which tool (search, Code Interpreter, DALL-E) to use based on your prompt, without you selecting one manually.

Canvas — ChatGPT's side-by-side editing workspace for collaborative writing and coding.

Chatbot — A software application that conducts conversation with users. ChatGPT started as a chatbot but has evolved into a broader AI platform.

Codex — OpenAI's agentic coding tool, separate from but related to ChatGPT's Code Interpreter capabilities.

Code Interpreter — ChatGPT's ability to write and execute Python code to analyze data, create charts, process files, and perform calculations.

Connectors (MCP) — Integrations that let ChatGPT access data from external services like Google Drive, Gmail, Stripe, and others. MCP (Model Context Protocol) is an open standard originally developed by Anthropic and adopted by OpenAI.

Context window — The maximum amount of text (prompts and responses combined) that a language model can process at once. When conversations exceed the context window, earlier content is no longer accessible to the model.

Custom GPT — A specialized version of ChatGPT configured with specific instructions, knowledge files, and tool access for a particular purpose.

Custom Instructions — Standing directions you give ChatGPT about who you are and how you'd like it to respond, applied to every conversation.

DALL-E — OpenAI's image generation model, integrated into ChatGPT for creating images from text descriptions.

Deep Research — A ChatGPT feature that conducts multi-step research across many web sources and produces structured, cited reports.

Fine-tuning — The process of further training an AI model on specific data to improve its performance on particular tasks.

GPT (Generative Pre-trained Transformer) — The family of language models that powers ChatGPT. "Generative" means it generates text; "pre-trained" means it learned from large amounts of data before being made available to users; "Transformer" refers to the underlying architecture.

GPT Store — A directory of Custom GPTs created by OpenAI and community members, browsable and usable within ChatGPT.

Hallucination — When an AI model generates information that sounds plausible but is factually incorrect, invented, or unsupported.

Large Language Model (LLM) — A type of AI model trained on vast amounts of text data that can understand and generate human language. ChatGPT is powered by LLMs.

Memory — ChatGPT's ability to retain information you share across conversations, allowing it to personalize responses over time.

Model — The underlying AI system that processes your input and generates responses. Different models (GPT-5.3, GPT-5.4) have different capabilities.

Multimodal — The ability to process multiple types of input — text, images, audio, video — within a single system. ChatGPT is multimodal.

OpenAI — The company that creates and operates ChatGPT. Founded in 2015, headquartered in San Francisco.

Parameter — An internal setting in a neural network that's adjusted during training. More parameters generally means greater capability. Modern LLMs have hundreds of billions of parameters.

Prompt — The text you type into ChatGPT. Also called a query, input, or message.

Prompt engineering — The practice of crafting effective prompts to get desired outputs from AI models.

Projects — ChatGPT's organizational feature for grouping related conversations with shared context, files, and instructions.

RLHF (Reinforcement Learning from Human Feedback) — A training technique where human evaluators rate AI responses, and the model learns to produce responses that humans prefer.

Sora — OpenAI's video generation model, integrated into ChatGPT for creating video clips from text descriptions.

Study Mode — A ChatGPT feature designed for learning, using Socratic questioning and interactive testing rather than simply providing answers.

Sycophancy — An AI model's tendency to agree with the user or tell them what they want to hear, even when the user is incorrect.

Temporary Chat — A per-conversation privacy mode where the conversation isn't saved to history, doesn't create memories, and isn't used for model training.

Token — The basic unit of text that a language model processes. One token is roughly three-quarters of an English word. "ChatGPT is helpful" is about 4 tokens.

Training — The process of teaching an AI model by exposing it to large amounts of data so it learns patterns and relationships.

Training data — The text, images, and other information used to train an AI model. ChatGPT's training data includes books, websites, articles, and code.

Voice Mode — ChatGPT's spoken conversation feature, allowing real-time voice interaction with natural-sounding speech.

Appendix E: What's New in 2026

A timeline of major ChatGPT developments, for readers who want to see how the platform reached its current state.

The GPT-5 Era

August 2025 — GPT-5 launches. OpenAI's strongest model to date — major gains in writing, coding, and reasoning, with fewer hallucinations. Less sycophantic than its predecessors.

Late 2025 — GPT-5.1 family. GPT-5.1 Instant and GPT-5.1 Thinking establish the tiered model approach within the GPT-5 generation.

Early 2026 — GPT-5.3 Instant. Rolls out as the default model for all ChatGPT users. GPT-5.3 introduces auto-switching — a single model that routes requests to the appropriate capability (search, code, images) without user intervention.

March 2026 — GPT-5.4 Thinking. The frontier reasoning model, with improvements in spreadsheet creation, frontend code, slideshow generation, complex math, document understanding, and agentic workflows.

March 2026 — GPT-5.1 deprecated. GPT-5.1 models removed from ChatGPT as GPT-5.3 and 5.4 supersede them.

Major Features

January 2025 — Operator launches (Pro only). OpenAI's first agentic feature, letting ChatGPT complete tasks in a web browser. Initially limited to Pro subscribers.

July 2025 — Operator becomes Agent Mode. Rebranded and expanded to Plus and Business users. Built directly into ChatGPT rather than existing as a separate product.

October 2025 — Atlas browser launches. ChatGPT's AI-native browser ships on macOS, putting the assistant alongside users as they browse.

Late 2025 — Study Mode. An interactive tutoring experience that uses Socratic questioning, scaffolded explanations, and knowledge checks rather than simply handing over answers.

January 2026 — ChatGPT Go tier. A new $8/month plan launches globally — an affordable middle ground between Free and Plus.

February 2026 — Ads on Free tier. Advertising begins appearing for Free and Go users in the United States.

March 2026 — Interactive Learning. ChatGPT adds interactive visual modules for 70+ math and science topics, letting users manipulate formulas and variables in real time.

March 2026 — Legacy Deep Research removed. The older Deep Research experience is retired in favor of the current, improved version.

Platform Changes

Customizable Personalities. ChatGPT gains personality options — Cynic, Robot, Listener, and Nerd — letting users choose how it interacts. Currently text-only; voice support planned.

MCP Connectors. Enterprise connectors expand to include Amplitude, Fireflies, Vercel, Monday.com, Stripe, Hex, Egnyte, Semrush, and others.

macOS Voice Changes. The voice experience in the macOS app is simplified in January 2026. Voice continues on chat.com, iOS, Android, and Windows.

Superapp Development. OpenAI announces plans to merge ChatGPT, Codex, and Atlas into a single desktop application.

Pricing Evolution

Tier	Price	Key Change
Free	$0	Ads added (US, Feb 2026)
Go	$8/mo	New tier (Jan 2026)
Plus	$20/mo	Stable
Pro	$200/mo	Stable
Business	$25/user/mo	MCP connectors added

Tier	Price	Key Change
Enterprise	Custom	Expanded compliance features

What to Watch For

The pace of change shows no signs of slowing. Areas likely to see meaningful developments in the coming months:

- **The superapp:** Unifying ChatGPT, Codex, and Atlas into a single experience
- **Atlas on more platforms:** Windows, iOS, and Android versions
- **Agent Mode expansion:** More capable, more autonomous, better integrated with external services
- **Model improvements:** Each generation brings meaningful gains in reasoning, accuracy, and capability
- **Enterprise features:** Deeper integrations, more connectors, expanded compliance
- **Multimodal evolution:** Better image, video, and audio capabilities

Stay current by following OpenAI's blog (openai.com/blog) and checking the release notes in ChatGPT's help center.

Appendix F: Resources and Further Reading

Official OpenAI Resources

- **ChatGPT:** chat.com
- **Help Center:** help.openai.com
- **OpenAI Blog:** openai.com/blog
- **Release Notes:** help.openai.com/en/articles/6825453-chatgpt-release-notes
- **System Status:** status.openai.com
- **Community Forum:** community.openai.com
- **API Documentation:** platform.openai.com/docs
- **Safety & Privacy:** openai.com/safety

Staying Current

ChatGPT changes constantly. These resources help you keep up:

Newsletters: - Ben's Bites — Daily AI news digest - The Neuron — AI news for non-technical readers - Superhuman by Zain Kahn — AI productivity tips

YouTube Channels: - All About AI — Tutorials and feature walkthroughs - Matt Wolfe — AI tool reviews and news - The AI Advantage — Practical AI workflows

Podcasts: - Hard Fork (The New York Times) — Technology and AI news - The AI Daily Brief — Short daily AI updates - Latent Space — Technical but accessible AI discussions

Books for Further Learning

On AI and its implications: - *Co-Intelligence* by Ethan Mollick — How to think about AI as a collaborator - *The Coming Wave* by Mustafa Suleyman — AI's broader societal impact

On prompting and AI productivity: - *ChatGPT: The Power User Guide (2026 Edition)* — The companion to this book, covering advanced techniques, systems thinking, and prompt engineering

On the other AI assistants: - *Claude: The Definitive Guide (2026 Edition)* — Anthropic's AI assistant - *Claude Code: The Power User Guide (2026 Edition)* — For developers using AI-assisted coding

The above three titles are published by Finnoybu Press.

Community and Learning

- **Reddit:** r/ChatGPT — User discussions, tips, and discoveries
- **Discord:** Multiple AI communities exist; search for "AI" or "ChatGPT" on Discord's server directory
- **LinkedIn:** Follow AI thought leaders for professional perspectives on AI adoption
- **X (Twitter):** Follow @OpenAI for official updates

For Developers

If you want to build with OpenAI's technology:

- **API Quickstart:** platform.openai.com/docs/quickstart
- **Cookbook:** github.com/openai/openai-cookbook — Code examples and best practices
- **Developer Forum:** community.openai.com

For Educators

- **OpenAI's Education Hub:** openai.com/education
- **Teaching with AI (MIT RAISE):** raise.mit.edu — Resources for integrating AI into curriculum while maintaining academic integrity
- **AI Literacy Frameworks (AI4K12):** ai4k12.org — The "Five Big Ideas in AI" framework for teaching AI literacy at K–12 grade levels

Feedback and Updates

This book is updated periodically to reflect changes in ChatGPT's features and capabilities. For the latest edition and errata:

press.finnoybu.org

Found an error or have a suggestion? Contact:

press@finnoybu.org

www.ingramcontent.com/pod-product-compliance
Ingram Content Group UK Ltd.
Pitfield, Milton Keynes, MK11 3LW, UK
UKHW061826190726
13853UKWH00009B/2454